THE GOSPEL
ACCORDING TO
St.Paul

Hubert Richards

THE LITURGICAL PRESS
Collegeville, Minnesota 56321

Great Wakering, Essex

Acknowledgements

Except where stated, scriptural quotations are taken from *The Jerusalem Bible* (copyright © 1966, 1967 and 1968 by Darton, Longman and Todd Ltd and Doubleday and Company Inc. Used by permission of the publisher). On a few occasions the author has felt free to make minor changes for the sake of precision.
Thanks are due to the Oxford University Press for permission to quote from Alan T. Dale's translation of the New Testament, *New World* © Oxford University Press 1967.

Thanks are also due to Mayhew-McCrimmon Ltd for permission to reproduce 'Deep, deep' (p.134) which first appeared in *Heart of a Rose* by Hubert Richards.

First published by Darton, Longman and Todd Ltd
This revised and enlarged edition published 1990 by
McCrimmon Publishing Co Ltd
10–12 High Street, Great Wakering, Essex SS3 0EQ

© 1990 H.J.Richards

McCrimmons
ISBN 0 85597 451 6

Liturgical Press
ISBN 0–8146–2057–4

Cover design by Nick Snode
Lithographic artwork by McCrimmon Publishing Co Ltd.
Typesetting by Fleetlines, Southend.
Typeset in Aster, 11 on 12 point
Printed by Black Bear Press Ltd., Cambridge

Contents

This book is for Clare,
who lives her theology instead of writing about it

1. In Praise of Paul

Whenever I hear the epistles of Paul read out in the liturgy, I am filled with joy. I thrill every time I hear his call ringing out. My heart beats faster every time I recognise his voice. He seems to come into our very midst, and to be speaking in this church.

What distresses me is that some people hardly know Paul at all. Some know him so little that they can't even tell you how many epistles he wrote! They plead their lack of education. What they ought to admit is that they've never bothered to take up his writings and read them.

If I'm regarded as a learned man, it's not because I'm brainy. It's simply because I have such a love for Paul that I've never left off reading him. He has taught me all I know. And I want you to listen carefully to what he has to teach you. You don't need to do anything else.

Just search and you will find, just
knock and the door will be opened.

So spoke Chrysostom in the fourth century. His enthusiasm for Paul has been echoed by many other admirers down the years. Most of those who have accepted that invitation to take Paul's writings into their hands have ended up by becoming his fans.

Yet no one would describe Paul as ever having become popular. Somehow, alongside the spontaneous accolades, the intervening centuries have consistently given him a bad press. Perhaps the history of theological controversy has been one of the contributing factors. Certainly it is this that has instilled into most Roman Catholics the unspoken suspicion that Paul

John Fisher

was really a Protestant. With the result that in the Roman Catholic Church, alongside the countless parish churches dedicated to St Joseph and to the Guardian Angels, I can number on my fingers the ones which are dedicated to St Paul.

A certain type of popular writing has misrepresented Paul even further, and effectively persuaded people that he was a dour, unsympathetic misogynist, who twisted the simple and kindly message of Jesus into a cruel and complicated religion.

But his public image has perhaps suffered most from the extracts from his writings which for centuries were laid down as the 'epistles' to be read out at the Sunday service. Apart from two or three favourites, they seemed to be preoccupied with arguments that had little to do with the people who had to sit and listen to them. Jews and Gentiles, Macedonia and Achaia, Sarah and Hagar, spirit and flesh, law and grace – the man in the pew suffered from them all because they were part of the sacred ritual. They scarcely gave him the feeling, especially if he had to endure them in the Douay or Authorised version, that he wanted to rush home and read the rest.

There is no denying that Paul's writings can be complex. Nor can we presume that everything he wrote about will necessarily be relevant to our twentieth century. He was dealing, after all, with problems arising out of a world very different to the one we live in. Yet the fact remains that all those who have had the patience to understand those problems and to unravel those complexities have maintained that the labour was more than worth while.

Because what emerges from such a task is not simply the reconstruction of a past age but of a vision of Christianity such as once quite literally changed the face of the world.

Is it perhaps Paul's style that puts people off him? They would not be the first to discover that he does not always read as smoothly as one would wish. A first-century writer said: 'Our beloved brother Paul writes according to the wisdom given him... in his letters in which there are some things hard to understand' (2 Peter 3:16).

The difficulty therefore was felt from the beginning. Paul's letters are obviously not carefully planned theological treatises, otherwise one might have the right to complain about his lack of clarity. They are mostly emergency writings, written off the cuff to answer special needs. Paul did not sit down to write them as one might sit down to write an article. He was clearly rampaging up and down the room, 'giving out' at dictation speed. He can digress for a couple of paragraphs – or even a couple of chapters – before coming back to the matter in hand. The end product is passionate, fiery and tempestuous, and does not make for easy reading. But it does put us in touch with the man himself, not merely with a public image of himself that he wanted to project. To read a letter of his is to have the most vivid impression, as Chrysostom noted, of the man being present in the room and speaking.

Is the man himself worth knowing? There is a second century description of him in the pages of the apocryphal *Acts of Paul*: 'Small of stature, balding, bow legs, large eyes, eyebrows meeting, nose slightly hooked.' In a work which otherwise goes out of its way to praise him, this description is so unflattering that it bears the mark of being taken from life. Yet it goes on: 'His appearance was full of grace: sometimes he looked more like an angel than a man.' This strange mixture – of a physically unimpressive man who was yet singularly impressive – fits the picture given by Chrysostom too who refers to him as 'five feet high, but with a reach beyond the stars'.

And a quotation taken straight from his own writings bears out the same supposition, that he must have been an extraordinary mass of contradictions. I have ventured to paraphrase the quotation because the version with which people are familiar is apparently so pointless, with its talk of 'journeyings often', and 'speaking as one less wise', and 'whether in the body or out of the body I know not God knoweth', and its curious list of apparently unrelated events. In actual fact it is a perfect vignette of Paul with his heart on his sleeve. It reveals him as few other pages can.

He is trying to defend himself against Christian missionaries who are spreading calumnies and lies about his missionary work in Corinth a few years earlier. They have suggested that he is insincere and inconstant, arrogant and despotic, and only interested in the money that preaching the gospel can bring him. Since the Corinthians are half beginning to believe these slanders, Paul is forced to defend himself. He has to say: 'If they are comparing me to themselves, I can show you that I don't come out of it too badly.' But he hates it. He keeps on repeating how embarrassed he is by this game of 'Anything you can do I can do better.' Yet if his critics are doing it, he cannot do other than follow suit. If Corinth is so easily bowled over by their self-recommendations, then Paul must imitate them. He writes:

I apologise for what I'm about to do. Please don't think that I've gone mad. Or do think so, if you like, as long as you realise that I have no choice, otherwise my rivals will sweep you off your feet. I've got to be in on this game too.

In any case, you Corinthians are obviously quite happy to put up with this sort of tomfoolery, because you have such superior intelligences that you can't possibly be taken in by it!

Well, I say that if you can put up with them, even though they're making slaves of you, even though they're living on your money, even though they're taking you in, even though they're only using you to climb higher, even though they're insulting you – I say, if you can put up with the boasting of people like that, then I'm sure that you can put up with mine for a bit, even though I have to confess to my shame, that I'll never match them as slavemasters, spongers and slanderers.

However if there *is* going to be a boasting competition (I must be off my head to talk like this), I insist on joining in. Let's begin.

They back themselves up by appealing to their origins. Right, I'll do so too. They boast that they belong to the Jewish nation. Well, so do I. They claim to be part of God's Chosen People. So am I. They claim to be descendants of Abraham and therefore the heirs of God's promise. I'm that too. They claim to be servants of Christ. Ah! now there I can go one better (this is a silly game, but you asked for it). Here's my list of qualifications:

I have sweated harder than they have.

I have served longer prison sentences than they have.

I have been beaten up more often than they have.

I have risked my life more often than they have.

From the Jews I have had five floggings – the thirty-nine regulation stripes.

From the Romans I have had three floggings – and they, as you know, set no limits. This in spite of my Roman citizenship, which was supposed to protect me from such an eventuality.

I have once even been stoned, to the extent that people were satisfied that I wouldn't get up again.

I have been three times shipwrecked, and left adrift

twenty-four hours on the open sea as a castaway.

I have covered eight thousand miles in my missionary journeys, each one of them full of danger: unbridged rivers to cross, bandits on the road, and the constant hostility not only of the pagans – this was only to be expected – but of my own brother Jews as well. It's been danger all the way: in the cities, out in the open country, on the high seas. Not to mention the ever present danger of fellow Christians ruining my work from the inside (I don't need to spell out names!)

I have sweated, I have been weary, I've spent sleepless nights, I've suffered from hunger and thirst and missed meals, I've suffered from the cold and lack of adequate clothing.

I could go on, but I won't bore you any further. I'll just remind you that, on top of all this, I am constantly crushed, day after day, by my anxious concern for all the converts I have made in the Middle East, from Antioch to Athens, from the Black Sea to the Mediterranean. If any one of them feels a scruple, I feel it too. If any of them fail in their Christian vocation, I am myself tortured by the pain of it.

But look! This is too embarrassing for words. I really can't go on in this strain. If I am forced to blow my own trumpet, then I shall just have to play a tune which humiliates me.

Eastern Daily Press

You can laugh at me if you like, but I really can't go on saying what a good boy am I!

I swear that this really happened. A few years ago the Jews at Damascus were out for my blood, and asked King Aretas to help them catch me by posting guards. The only way that I was able to get away was being let down through a window in the town walls, in a clothes basket mind you! There, that's the sort of dignified exit I can boast about! Go on, laugh at me!

No! As you were! Here's me refusing to sing my own praises, and there are my rivals trying to impress you with the visions and revelations and ecstasies they've been favoured with. So be it! Let's get on to the visions. This is even more embarrassing of course, but I must show you that even on this score I don't fall behind them. Now that we're back on the boasting game, let's end up with something really good! Though perhaps I'd better talk about it in the third person, to avoid this embarrassing repetition of 'I, I, I'.

This happened fourteen years ago. A certain man, a Christian whom I know very well (!), had an ecstasy and was caught up in heaven itself. Whether his body went with him or stayed here on earth, I have no idea. All that I'm certain of is that he really entered the presence of God, that it was not a dream or fantasy, and that there he heard mysteries so sublime that there are no human words to express them. There now! Isn't that something to boast about?

But no, let's stop this boasting. If I must speak about myself, I'd rather speak about my most embarrassing moments.

Mind you, if I wanted to boast, I'd be perfectly justified. I've got plenty to boast about, without needing to have recourse – as some do – to fiction! But I won't bore you. I hate it anyway. I want you to take me exactly as you find me, not as I make myself out to be. So I *will* tell you about my embarrassing moments.

Someone made quite sure that I wouldn't get a swelled head about these mystical experiences of mine – God. He let the devil torture me. He let my fellow Jews, my own flesh and blood, be a constant thorn in my side. And this constant humiliation was so unbearable that three times I asked God to free me from it. But he only replied: 'My grace is strong enough for you to bear it. The fact that it crushes you and leaves you weak will only make it the more obvious that it is my strength, not yours, which is keeping you going.'

There! That is the reason I don't mind mentioning things which make people laugh at me, even this humiliating persecution from my own people. I don't in the least mind being an object of ridicule, because that only makes it all the more obvious that if my preaching is successful, it is not due to my ridiculous self, but to the power of Christ living in me. I'm really quite glad that I get battered with persecution, hardship and insults. The weaker I am, the more powerful Christ is in me.

That was a stupid boasting competition! But you drove me to it. In fact *you* should have been doing the boasting for me. But since you didn't, I had to show you myself that I don't fall short of these supermen of yours. If they tell you they can work miracles, you will remember, won't you, that you've had actual tangible evidence of the miracles that I worked among you! There is only one point on which I have to admit that I don't match up to them – the fact that, unlike them, I've accepted no money from you. I hope you will forgive me this! (2 Corinthians 11:16 – 12:13, author's translation)

Can anyone fail to be attracted by a Paul such as this? Would it be in spite of the self-contradictions he reveals, or because of them? A Paul who is so concerned for his friends that he has stepped right out of his character to throw his weight around; a Paul who is so embarrassed by the whole thing that he is blushing all over.

But of course that sketch of him represents only one chapter out of his writings. There are 86 others.

FOR DISCUSSION

1. In the long quotation from 2 Corinthians above, what verse or verses speak to you most deeply?

2. What do you find most attractive about Paul? And what most off-putting?

3. Many recent Jewish studies, while they are beginning to warm to Jesus, cannot stomach Paul. What do you think is the reason for this?

2. A Postcard to Philemon

One of the 86 other chapters Paul wrote is known as the epistle to Philemon. 'Epistle' is a rather grandiose name for what is really little more than a postcard.

POST CARD
THE ADDRESS TO BE WRITTEN ON THIS SIDE

ΠΑΥΛΟΣ ΦΙΛΗΜΟΝΙ

ΕΝ ΚΟΛΟΣΣΑΙΣ

John Fisher

Philemon was one of the outstanding citizens in the town of Colossae, and he became a Christian under the influence of Paul's preaching there. Towards the end of his life Paul wrote to the Christians in Colossae from his prison in Rome, and took the opportunity to put this private note to Philemon in the same post. It's survival in the New Testament is possibly due to the fact that Philemon was the first to make a full collection of Paul's letters, and included this personal letter at the end of the collection. Certainly the fact that he published it suggests that it made a deep impression on him.

At Colossae, Philemon had owned a pagan slave named Onesimos. The name means 'useful', and since the word is twice used in the letter as a pun, a modern translation would have to render it something like 'Andy. In any case, Onesimos had proved rather useless: he had stolen Philemon's savings and made off to Rome, hoping like many thieves since to get lost in the 'Smoke'.

He had not reckoned with the fact that Paul was in Rome at the time. House-prisoner though he was, Paul not only established contact with him but made a Christian of him too. 'In fact', he tells Philemon, 'he's been most 'andy to me because he's been able to run errands for me round the town while I've been housebound.'

However, there is no question of Onesimos staying in Rome in Paul's service. Paul has no right to keep him; he is still Philemon's property, and if Philemon wants to apply the full rigour of the current law on robbery he can have him put to death. As Paul packs off the slave to his master, his covering note simply asks Philemon to consider the situation carefully. Onesimos is still technically his slave, but in Christ Jesus he has also become his brother. Here is Alan Dale's translation of this short letter:

My dear Philemon, friend and fellow-worker,

When I am saying my prayers and I come to your name, I always thank God for you. People often tell me how much you love and trust Jesus, and how much you love and trust the friends of Jesus too. This love and trust is something we all share together; and sharing it together has shown us how much Jesus means to us, how good now it is to be alive. Your love has meant a lot to me and made me very happy. And what's more, you've cheered the hearts of all the friends of Jesus, too, my brother.

Now, I've got something I want you to do. I wouldn't be afraid, as a friend of Jesus, just to tell you what your duty is, and leave it at that. But I'd rather appeal to the love we both have for Jesus and one another. I'm an old man now, you know, and, what's more, I'm a prisoner as well for the sake of Jesus; and I'm appealing to you for my boy.

It's Onesimos I'm talking about – I became like a father to him here in prison.[1] I'm sending him home to you – and sending my heart with him. I should have liked to keep him here with me; he could have been a great help, and taken your place by my side, prisoner as I am for the Good News. But I wouldn't do anything unless you said Yes. I know, of course, that you'd do the right thing; but I want it to be your choice, not mine.

[1] Dale points out that Paul has here made a pun on the name of Onesimos which has not been translated.

He was perhaps taken away from you for a short time so that you could have him back again to stay with you always – no longer a slave but something far better than a slave, a real brother. He is a brother to me now; and he will be much more a brother to you, both as a man and a friend of Jesus.

If you think of me as your partner, welcome him as you would welcome me.

If he's done you a wrong or he's in debt to you, put it down to my account.

I, PAUL, WRITE THIS WITH MY OWN HAND – I WILL PAY YOU BACK.

I don't need to remind you that you owe your very self to me. Now I come to think of it, I'd like to make something out of this[2] – the sort of thing Jesus would make out of it. Cheer me up, as the real Christian you are.

I know you'll do what I ask. I wouldn't have written to you otherwise. In fact, I know you'll do more than I ask.

And while you are about it, get a room ready for me. I know you've been praying for me; I hope God will answer your prayers and give me back to you.

Remember me to Apphia our sister; and to Archippus our fellow-soldier; and to all the friends of Jesus who meet in your home.

Epaphras is a prisoner here with me; he sends you his best wishes. So do the others who are working here with me – Mark, Aristarchus, Demas and Dr. Luke.

How real Jesus has made God's love and peace! May the graciousness of Jesus be with you all.

Paul (a prisoner here in the cause of Jesus) and Timothy. (*New World*, Oxford 1967, p. 326ff.)

A commentator remarks that if the first years of Christianity had produced nothing else but this in way of written documents, one would know that a great new thing had come into the world. Chrysostom writes:

What stone could have failed to be softened by these words? There never was anything like the compassion and loving kindness of blessed Paul.

What is so striking about the letter is not simply the exquisite courtesy with which it is written, nor simply the delicate

---

2 There is another more explicit pun on the name of Onesimos here: 'You could do something very 'andy for me.'

balance between playfulness and profound spirituality. It is above all its attitude to slavery. It is this that is new in the world of A.D. 61. According to Tacitus, a Roman prefect was assassinated by one of his slaves in that year. Roman law stipulated the execution not only of the slave, but of the whole slave-household with him. Four hundred slaves were crucified.

The grandeur of the gospel that Paul and others preached was that it was able to transform such a world. Not that Paul himself necessarily realised the logical implications of the good news he preached. Yet by receiving both slave and master into the same community, by showing them that in Christ they were brothers, he created an atmosphere in which slavery could eventually no longer breathe. This is not to say that there have been no slavemasters who called themselves Christians – but presumably they never read or understood the letters of Paul.

FOR DISCUSSION

1. Paul's greetings to Philemon on p. 14 are very warm and packed with Christian references. Why do you think we no longer use this sort of language with our Christian friends? Is this style too impossibly dated for us to copy today?

2. Why do you think Paul condoned Philemon's use of slave labour, instead of condemning it outright?

3. Is there something sectarian about Paul's advice to treat Onesimos as a brother now that he is a fellow Christian?

3. Jitters in Salonika (Thessalonians)

Of the two letters of St. Paul which have come down to us, the two he wrote about the year A.D. 50 to the Christians at Thessalonica were the first. This places them among the earliest writings which now make up the New Testament; they are far older than any of our existing gospels.

Background

Thessalonica – or Salonika as it is now called – is an important seaport in northern Greece. In Paul's time it ranked second

only to Athens, and was capital of the northern half of Greece, or Macedonia.

Paul had visited it just a few months earlier, on the missionary journey which had first brought the gospel out of Asia Minor into Europe; the people of Salonika had been among the first Europeans to whom he had preached. Both letters mention the enthusiasm with which Paul's Jewish and pagan audience had welcomed the Good News of Jesus Christ, in spite of the opposition mounted against him by a section of the Jewish community. In fact both letters make this the theme of their opening lines:

> We always mention you in our prayers and thank God for you all, and constantly remember before God our Father how you have shown your faith in action, worked for love, and persevered through hope in our Lord Jesus Christ.
>
> We know, brothers, that God loves you and you have been chosen, because when we brought the Good News to you, it came to you not only as words, but as power and as the Holy Spirit and as utter conviction. And you observed the sort of life we lived when we were with you, which was for your instruction, and you were led to become imitators of us, and of the Lord; and it was with the joy of the Holy Spirit that you took to the gospel, in spite of the great opposition all round you. This has made you the great example to all believers in Macedonia and Greece since it was from you that the word of the Lord started to spread – and not only throughout Macedonia and Greece, for the news of your faith in God has spread everywhere. We do not need to tell other people about it: other people tell us. (1 Thessalonians 1:2–9)

> We feel we must be continually thanking God for you, brothers; quite rightly, because your faith is growing so wonderfully and the love that you have for one another never stops increasing; and among the churches of God we can take special pride in your constancy and faith under all the persecutions and troubles you have to bear. It all shows that God's judgement is just, and the purpose of it is that you may be found worthy of the Kingdom of God; it is for the sake of this that you are suffering now. (2 Thessalonians 1:3–5)

The persecution mentioned in both excerpts, fierce as it was for the Christians of Salonika, was fiercer still for Paul. He had only barely managed to establish a Christian community when he was forced to leave; it was a pattern he finally came to accept wherever he went. So he had made his way southwards through Greece to Athens, and finally to Corinth. When engaged in teaching there he made plans several times to return north to see how his converts were doing. Circumstances – Paul calls them the machinations of Satan himself – prevented him. Eventually, in desperation, and anxious to know what was happening, he sent one of his party, Timothy, to find out. Then he sat back ('dead worried' he says in 1 Thessalonians 3:8) holding his breath about what Timothy would bring back.

UNRWA photo by J.Madvo

Timothy's news was, on the whole, encouraging. The persecution had continued unabated, but it had not shaken the little community. Short as his stay among them had been, Paul had instilled into them a faith and a constancy which was proof against all attacks.

But there was disturbing news too: Paul's professional conduct had been criticised. Paul was not, of course, the only Christian missionary touring the Middle East in the year A.D. 50. There were dozens of them, varying in merit. Many were sincere enough, others quite unashamedly on the make. And Paul's enemies in Salonika, finding they could make no impact on the Christians by picking holes in what he had taught them, began to pick holes in him. Was he any better than these impostors? Was he not simply in this business for the money that could be made out of it? Why had he never returned to Salonika? Didn't it prove that he had no real concern for the Christians there?

There were other matters too in Timothy's report which gave Paul furrowed brows. There was considerable confusion in Salonika on sexual morality. Given the pagan background from which so many of the Christian converts came, with its toleration and even encouragement of every kind of license, and given the short time that Paul had had to instruct them, could he be a little more explicit about what was expected of a Christian?

But there was more confusion still on the subject of the Coming of Christ – a topic which apparently Paul had emphasised heavily in his preaching at Salonika. He was to modify his views later, but in his earlier preaching he saw Jesus' earthly ministry as only partially fulfilling God's promises. These would not be completely fulfilled except by something far more decisive – a Coming of Christ which had about it a power and a glory which none could dispute. To this Coming Paul had directed the hopes and aspirations of his listeners in Salonika, urging them to live in daily expectation of it.

Timothy's news was that they were beginning to ask, not unnaturally, what the delay was. Some of the older people had died: how was it that Paul had not warned them of this possibility? Had these people missed the Coming of Christ? When was it to be expected now? Could he be a little more explicit on this point too?

Paul wrote his first letter to Salonika in response to the situation just described. It is, in the first place, a sigh of relief ('I breathed again' he says) that his converts have not thrown their new-found faith overboard. Next, he wants to thank God for their constancy under persecution and to defend himself against the slanders spread by his enemies. And finally he tries to answer the questions he had been asked, especially about the coming of Christ.

The letter was, if anything, too successful. On hearing its contents, many of his converts gave up their jobs, convinced that the Coming of Christ was due within days! To be fair to Paul, this was not entirely his fault. There is a reference in the Salonika correspondence to the fact that others apart from Paul were interested in a 'Coming of Christ in Our Time'. Some had claimed a heavenly revelation to this effect, others an interview with Paul claiming this to be his opinion. There was even a forged letter circulating, allegedly from Paul, stating that the Coming had already taken place. In this atmosphere, Paul's moderate enough letter had only excited Salonika to fever pitch.

Within months, therefore, Paul was back in his study, dictating a second letter to Salonika.[1] Its aim to clear up the misunderstanding. 'I did not mean as soon as all that,' he tells his readers. 'You know as well as I do the signs that must precede his coming, and they haven't even started yet.' And to guard against future forgeries, Paul signed the dictated letter in his own handwriting. He made it a rule for all future letters.

Paul and his correspondents

So much for the setting of Paul's correspondence with Salonika, and its contents. But much more needs to be said about the two letters. And first about the light they throw on Paul himself.

These letters are the earliest Paul wrote. Obviously his later correspondence reveals much about Paul's relationship with his converts, but none of it ever reaches the level of tenderness expressed here. I quoted above from his letter to Corinth, which speaks of his daily overwhelming anxiety for all those to whom he has preached the gospel. That loving and affectionate concern shines out of every line of these early writings of his.

His approach to these simple working folk might have been that of the stern taskmaster, laying down the law with threats of hellfire. It clearly wasn't: he had worn himself out, and continued to do so, to ensure that they heard the good news of the gospel, and understood it, and lived it. The reaction to the news that some of his converts were wavering in their new-found faith might have been a shrug of annoyance and disappointment. It clearly wasn't: the mere possibility tore his heart out. They were the children for whom he felt a father's responsibility, the babies for whom he felt a mother's concern. Timothy's news, in fact, threw him into the kind of turmoil in which he no longer knew where to turn for another image to express his feelings:

[1] 2 Thessalonians is here presumed to be genuinely from Paul. There are respectable scholars who find its understanding of the Coming of Christ sufficiently different from the view expressed in 1 Thessalonians to make them conclude that it must be a later work of Paul's disciples, writing in their master's name.

Barnaby's Picture Library

As an envoy of Christ, I could have come the heavy with you.
But I didn't. I was as unassuming as a babe while I was with
you. I was so concerned for you, I was a mother suckling her
children, wanting to give you not only God's gospel but my
whole self. That is how much I had come to love you. After
all, you are my brothers.

So far was I from trying to impose on you that (you
remember this, don't you) I worked among you day and
night till I was dropping, not only preaching God's gospel to
you, but supporting myself by my trade so as not to be a
burden to any of you. You remember too (and so does God)
how straightforward, how correct, how honest I was in all
my dealings with you, now that you had come to share my
faith. You can vouch for the fact that I was like a father to
each one of you, giving you heart, encouraging you, and
setting you an example of how to live a life worthy of the God
who has called you...

You will realise how little you've been out of my thoughts
when I tell you that from the first moment that I had to leave
you I felt like an orphaned child! Out of sight as you were,
but not out of mind, I was most anxious to see you again face
to face. I mean this. I myself, Paul, tried twice, no three
times, to come to see you. Only the demonic machinations of
my fellow Jews prevented me. Because you are my only hope
and joy and pride. (1 Thessalonians 2:6–20, author's
translation)

A child, a nursing mother, a brother, a father, an orphan –
could anyone else mix his metaphors like Paul?

Paul's loving concern for his correspondents emerges even
more strongly in the second of the two letters, where each of
the sections into which the letter naturally falls finishes with a
prayer. In a fraught situation, Paul's first reaction is to pray for
his people.

> We wish you grace and peace from God the Father and the
> Lord Jesus Christ. We feel we must be continually *thanking
> God* for you, brothers... (2 Thessalonians 1:2–3)

> Knowing of your sufferings, we *pray continually* that our God
> will make you worthy of his call, and by his power fulfil all
> your desires for goodness and complete all that you have
> been doing through faith, because in this way the name of
> Our Lord Jesus Christ will be glorified in you and you in him,
> by the grace of our God and the Lord Jesus Christ. (1:11–12)

> God will condemn all who refused to believe in the truth and
> chose wickedness instead. But we feel that we must be
> *continually thanking God* for you, brothers whom the Lord
> loves, because God chose you from the beginning to be saved
> by the sanctifying Spirit and by faith in the truth... *May our
> Lord* Jesus Christ himself, and God our Father... comfort you
> and strengthen you in everything good that you do and say.
> (2:12–17)

> We have every confidence that you are doing and will go on
> doing all that we tell you. *May the Lord* turn your hearts
> towards the love of God and the fortitude of Christ. (3:4–5)

> If anyone refuses to obey what I have written in this letter,
> take note of him, so that he will feel that he is in the wrong;
> though you are not to regard him as an enemy but as a
> brother in need of correction. *May the Lord* of Peace himself
> give you peace all the time and in every way... *May the grace
> of our Lord Jesus Christ* be with you all. (3:14–18)

In the moment of crisis, what it occurs to Paul to write to his
converts is one long prayer for them. All the other matters he
deals with, so one gets the impression, need to be dealt with
sure enough, but always in the context of his loving concern for
them before God. It is this, rather than the matters themselves,
that holds first place in his attention.

But perhaps Paul's relationship with his correspondents is most strikingly illustrated by the courtesy with which he treats them. Two phrases which keep returning in the two letters are most telling in this connection. He will not make his point by throwing his weight around, but by gracefully reminding his readers of what he presumes they already know. And he will not bludgeon them into holiness, but encourage them to it by respectfully saying again and again, 'You are trying very hard; I want you to try harder than ever.' Here is the first phrase:

> *You know* yourselves, my brothers, that our visit to you has not proved ineffectual. We had, *as you know*, been given rough treatment... (1 Thessalonians 2:1–2)

> *You know very well*, and we can swear it before God, that never at any time have our speeches been simply flattery. (2:5)

> *Let me remind you*, brothers, how hard we used to work... (2:9)

> *You are witnesses* that our treatment of you has been impeccably fair. *You can remember* how we treated every one of you. (2:10–11)

> *You have not forgotten* the instructions we gave you. (4:2)

> The Lord always punishes sins of that sort, *as we told you before* and assured you. (4:6)

> As for loving our brothers, there is *no need for anyone to write to you* about that, since you have learnt from God. (4:9)

> You will not be expecting us to write... since *you know very well*... (5:1–2)

> *You know* how you are supposed to imitate us... (2 Thessalonians 3:7)

And here is the second phrase:

> We urge you and appeal you in the Lord Jesus to make *more and more* progress in the kind of life that you are meant to live: the life that God wants, as you learnt from us, and *as you are already* living it. (1 Thessalonians 4:1)

You have learnt from God to love one another, and that is in fact *what you are doing*. However, we do urge you brothers, to *go on making even greater progress*. (4:10)

So give encouragement to each other, and *keep* strengthening one another, *as you do already*. (5:11)

Be considerate to those who are working among you as your teachers. Have an *ever and ever greater* respect for them. (5:12–13)

Pray for us that the Lord's message may spread quickly, and be received with honour *as it was among you*. (2 Thessalonians 3:1)

We have very confidence that you *are doing and will go on doing* all that we tell you. (3:4)

My brothers, *never grow tired* of doing what is right. (3:13)

Nothing in Paul's copious correspondence reveals so clearly the delicacy and courtesy of his dealings with people.

Paul the theologian

The personal tone which marks these extracts from the correspondence with Salonika is characteristic of all Paul's letters. They all have the same conversational note, and the same easy, freeflowing and unpredictable style.

This is not to say that he will not make an effort from time to time – in the great letter to Rome, for instance – to subdivide his material more carefully than he does in these light family pieces. But none of his letters could ever be called a treatise, a set theological essay. They all bear the mark, so obvious in the Salonika correspondence, of coming off the cuff. They are all occasional writings, dictated as it were in one breath, to the despair of anyone who has ever tried to write a paragraph entitled 'the plan of the epistle'.

One might be tempted to conclude from this that the letters must be rather superficial. How could one expect anything very deep in a correspondence which was thrown off so casually and which was so dependent on circumstances?

No conclusion could be more wrong. One doesn't have to read more than a few lines of any of the letters to appreciate the richness of Paul's thought. Paul can draw on enormous depths to illustrate the most off-hand remark. Take, for instance, the opening line of the first letter to Salonika:

From Paul, Silvanus and Timothy, to the church in Salonika
which is in God the Father and the Lord Jesus Christ;
wishing you grace and peace. (1 Thessalonians 1:1)

The phrase is simple enough, and to all appearances quite
innocent. Yet it is packed with a theology which, for someone
not immediately on Paul's wavelength, needs a fair amount of
unscrambling. To begin with, he reminds the Christians of
Salonika that they are not only the church *of* God, but that they
are *in* God, who has become the very atmosphere in which they
live and move. And he has become that for them because they
are *in* Christ. They are not merely followers or disciples of
Christ; they have been immersed in him, incorporated into
him, so that they draw on the very same source of life on which
he draws. And to be *in* Christ in that way is to be *in* God
because Christ is 'the Lord': he has acquired the very title that
the Old Testament reserved for God. In fact, for Paul, Christ is
so uniquely the entrance into the mystery of God that the two
words 'God' and 'Christ' can be governed by the same
preposition 'in'. He has not made any direct statement about
Christ, only an assumption, and it is all the more valuable for
being so unquestioned.

Finally, he wishes his readers
the 'grace' that Greeks wished
each other in their letters – only
he has charged it with the overtones which the word would
hold for Christians who had experienced the graciousness of
God revealed in the life and
death of Christ. And he wishes
them the 'peace' that Jews
wished each other – and this
word too has been enlarged to
include the Christian vision of
the harmony between God and
the human race brought about
by the ministry of Christ.

A theology as rich as this in
one verse? There is meat in
Paul's writings, and it needs
chewing, slowly.

Syndication International

Take, as another example, the words in which he concludes the first sentence of this letter. He is praising his correspondents for their constancy under persecution. He is telling them that their tenacity and steadfastness have edified Christians all over Greece: it is being talked about throughout the country, so that Paul can scarcely avoid mention of it cropping up again and again. And it is simply to round off this sentence that he paints an exquisite portrait of the Christian:

> The news of your faith in God has spread everywhere. We do not need to tell other people about it; the other people tell us how we started the work among you, how you broke with idolatry when you were converted to God and became servants of the real, living God; and how you are now waiting for Jesus, his Son, whom he raised from the dead to come from heaven to save us from the retribution which is coming. (1 Thessalonians 1:8–10)

It would be difficult to improve on this as a vignette of the Christian faith. Christians are those who know that without Christ their existence would be aimless, empty and without hope. What has changed their situation into one of hope and purpose is their experience of and share in the resurrection, in which they have with Christ made the breakthrough into the world of the ultimate reality of God. And in their certainty that what Christ has begun in them he will come to complete, Christians live a life full of expectancy, free from the guilt-ridden fear that haunts the rest of the human race.

It is obvious here Paul is not describing the Christian vocation of set purpose: his words are more in the nature of an aside. But his theology always comes through in that form. He is not consciously or deliberately elaborating a theology at all: it simply pours out of him quite effortlessly. And it clearly comes from a source which is very deep indeed.

Paul on Christian behaviour

The depth of Paul's theology can be best gauged from the sections in his letters that deal with Christian behaviour. When he gives advice Paul never uses the word 'law' in the way that we use, it meaning 'the police'. He never insists on a course of action because it is prescribed, because there is a commandment to that effect, or because authority says so. For him, more simply, Christian behaviour springs out of Christian belief. In his mind, morality is something not distinct from theology, but its natural fruit. Whatever the area of Christian living he has to deal with, his advice is very uncomplicated: 'Just realise what you *are*, and then *be* it.'

In his first letter, for instance, where he has been asked to give guidance on sexual morality, he begins on a thoroughly theological note:

> Finally, brothers, we urge you and appeal to you *in the Lord Jesus* to make more and more progress in the kind of life that you are meant to live... You have not forgotten the instructions we gave you *through the Lord Jesus*.
> (1 Thessalonians 4:1–2)

The advice is going to be based, in the first place, not on Paul's own example, not on his previous teaching, not on someone else's say-so, but on a far deeper reality. What he has to say to them only finds its full meaning *in* or *through* Christ, into whose risen body they have been incorporated. Christians must begin all their moral thinking at that level.

What, then, in detail, is the advice? Firstly:

> What God wants is for you all to be holy: He wants you to keep away from fornication, and each one of you to know how to use the body that belongs to him in a way that is holy and honourable, not giving way to selfish lust like the pagans who do not know God. (4:3–5)

Incorporation into the risen Christ has brought Christians into the presence of God. They are now holy, separated and consecrated, in something of the way that holy places are consecrated. Their attitude towards their own body therefore, and towards the bodies of others, must be marked with a sacred awe. They belong to God, and 'know' God with an intimacy not granted to all. Sexual immorality would be a sort of desecration. Next:

> God wants nobody at all ever to sin by taking advantage of a brother in these matters; the Lord always punishes sins of that sort, as we told you before and assured you. We have been called by God to be holy, not to be immoral. (4:6–7)

What Paul says about the incompatibility of fornication applies with even more force to adultery among Christians. For here the desecration is extended to another member of Christ's body, and for the Christian that should be almost unthinkable.

Hence the indirect reference to the coming of the Lord, when judgement will be passed to reveal the reality which the Christian now lives only by faith. Finally:

> Anyone who objects is not objecting to a human authority,
> but to God, who gives you his Holy Spirit. (4:8)

The trump card is kept to the end. The close kinship with God and with Christ of which Paul has been speaking is not merely formal or nominal. The Holy Spirit, the very Spirit of Christ, has been poured into the heart of Christians. Their body is, thenceforth, a kind of shrine of the Spirit of God. To violate it is, in the last analysis, a kind of sacrilege.

To sum up, the attitude of Christians to sex is to be based on the holiness of the God who has called them, on the judgement they await on the Coming of Christ, and on the Spirit who dwells in their heart. In other words, the great mysteries of Christianity – Trinity, Resurrection, Mystical Body, Parousia – these are not simply subjects to be studied but realities to be lived. Certainly for Paul, they constitute the very air he breathes. And he presumes that this goes for the housewives of Salonika too.

Paul's approach is far removed from the legalism which tries to make people good by act of parliament, and far removed

Barnaby's Picture Library

from the minimalism which asks how far you may go without actually sinning. As far as Paul is concerned, it is only the great mysteries at the heart of the Christian message which can truly enlarge and ennoble the soul. Christians who read his letters and do not let that insight influence their life are wasting their time.

Or shall we say with Paul, readers are letting it influence their life, only they must let it influence them more and more.

The Coming of Christ

I mentioned in the opening paragraphs of this chapter that the main object of Paul's correspondence with Salonika was to clarify his readers' ideas about the Coming of Christ, a topic on which he had clearly placed considerable emphasis in originally presenting Christianity to them. The topic is on his mind throughout the first letter. This is clear from the way he keeps alluding to it in passing, as if to say: 'Yes, I *am* coming to it'.

> We constantly remember before God our Father how you have shown your faith in action, worked for love, and persevered through *hope in our Lord Jesus Christ*.
> (1 Thessalonians 1:3)

> Other people tell us how you broke with idolatry... and how you are now *waiting for Jesus... to come* from heaven. (1:9–10)

> We appealed to you to live a life worthy of God, who is *calling you to share the glory of his kingdom*. (2:12)

> You will be the crown of which we shall be proudest *at the Coming of our Lord Jesus*. (2:19)

> May you be blameless in the sight of our God and Father *at the Coming of our Lord Jesus Christ*. (3:13)

When he finally does reach the topic, his explicit treatment of it is quite short. Some of the Christians in Salonika had been concerned not only that some of their loved ones had died – they had not catered for this possibility – but that they had thereby somehow been cheated of the Great Day. Paul reassures them. They are not to be worried by the mere fact of death, since incorporation into a risen Christ guarantees a share in his victory over death. Nor are they to have jitters about the delay in Christ's Coming: no one living a Christian life can possibly be taken by surprise. Here is what he writes:

We want you to be quite certain, brothers, about those who have died, to make sure you do not grieve about them, like the other people who have no hope. We believe that Jesus died and rose again, and that it will be the same for those who have died in Jesus: God will bring them with him.

We can tell you this from the Lord's own teaching, that any of us who are left alive until the Lord's Coming will not have any advantage over those who have died. At the trumpet of God, the voice of the archangel will call out the command and the Lord himself will come down from heaven; those who have died in Christ will be the first to rise, and then those of us who are still alive will be taken up in the clouds, together with them, to meet the Lord in the air. So we shall stay with the Lord for ever. With such thoughts as these you should comfort one another.

You will not be expecting us to write anything to you, brothers, about 'times and seasons', since you know very well that the Day of the Lord is going to come like a thief in the night. It is when people are saying, 'How quiet and peaceful it is' that the worst suddenly happens, as suddenly as labour pains come on a pregnant woman; and there will be no way for anybody to evade it.

But it is not as if you live in the dark, my brothers, for that Day to overtake you like a thief. No, you are all sons of light and sons of the day: we do not belong to the night or to darkness, so we should not go on sleeping, as everyone else does, but stay awake and sober. Night is the time for sleepers to sleep and drunkards to be drunk, but we belong to the day and should be sober; let us put on faith and love for a breastplate, and the hope of salvation for a helmet.

God never meant us to experience the Retribution, but to win salvation through our Lord Jesus Christ, who died for us so that, alive or dead, we should still live united to him. So give encouragement to each other, and keep strengthening each other, as you do already. (1 Thessalonians 4:13 – 5:11)

At first sight, Paul seems here to be offering a good deal of information about the kinds of things that may be expected to happen at the Last Day. And since that information is otherwise inaccessible, one might assume that it has been divinely revealed to him. On closer inspection, however, it becomes clear that he is offering no information at all. All the language he uses is borrowed language. The trumpet, the angelic voice, the divine command, the descent from the skies, the clouds – these are all symbols to be found in any contemporary piece of apocalyptic writing about the Day of the Lord. If Paul has simply taken over the accepted imagery of his times, the presumption is that he has no other information to work on. All that he is certain of is that 'we shall stay with the Lord for ever' and that 'we shall live united to God'. For the rest, he has no facts to go on, and he leaves his description deliberately vague.

Has he any more real information to offer in the second letter? Certainly he seems to go into far greater detail. The Christians of Salonika had apparently taken his letter to mean that the Coming of Christ could be expected any moment now, and had panicked. To restore order, Paul had to remind them of the things that must precede that Coming, of which there were as yet no signs. When these preliminaries began to take place they could start getting excited, not before. Here is what he writes this time:

> To turn now, brothers, to the Coming of our Lord Jesus Christ and how we shall all be gathered round him: please do not get excited too soon or alarmed by any prediction or rumour or any letter claiming to come from us, implying that the Day of the Lord has already arrived. Never let anyone deceive you in this way.
>
> It cannot happen until the Great Revolt has taken place, and the Rebel, the Lost One, has appeared. This is the Enemy, the one who claims to be so much greater than all that men call 'god', so much greater then anything that is worshipped, that he enthrones himself in God's sanctuary and claims that he is God. Surely you remember me telling you about this when I was with you? And you know, too, what is still holding him back before appearing before his appointed time. Rebellion is at its work already, but in secret, but the one who is holding it back has first to be removed before the Rebel appears openly. The Lord will kill him with the breath of his mouth and will annihilate him with his glorious appearance at his Coming.
>
> But at the Coming of the Rebel, Satan will set to work: there will be all kinds of miracles and a deceptive show of signs and portents, and everything evil that can deceive those who are bound for destruction because they would not

grasp the love of the truth which could have saved them. The reason why God is sending a power to delude them and make them believe what is untrue is to condemn all who refused to believe in the truth and chose wickedness instead.

But we feel that we must be continually thanking God for you, brothers whom the Lord loves, because God chose you from the beginning to be saved by the sanctifying Spirit and by faith in the truth. Through the Good News that we brought he called you to this so that you should share the glory of Our Lord Jesus Christ. Stand firm, then, brothers, and keep the traditions that we taught you, whether by word of mouth or by letter. (2 Thessalonians 2:1–15)

On the face of it, this scenario offers considerably more details than the first letter did, and the reader may suppose that here at last Paul is handing on divinely given information. For how else would he know about the Secret Rebellion already at work, and the Great Revolt which is soon to burst on the world? Or about the Rebel whose Coming will rival Christ's own, and the Obstacle which continues to hold him back until the appointed time?

The answer to those questions is simple. Paul 'knew' about these things from the same source from which he had already borrowed the trumpet, the angels and the clouds. The fact is that the apocalyptic literature of time, itself relying heavily on certain pages of the Old Testament prophets, spoke of the Day of the Lord in this kind of language, and it is not surprising that Paul should turn to it to speak of the Coming of Christ. Even Jesus, according to the gospel record, made use of this strange imagery to foretell nothing more earthshaking than the fall of Jerusalem within the next generation. In fact it is interesting that this discourse of Jesus as the gospel writers have interpreted it (Mark 13, Matthew 24, Luke 21) speaks as Paul does of a Revolt (the same Greek word is used), of the alarming and blasphemous miracles of a counterfeit Christ, and the final Coming of the Son of Man to gather together his elect.

To speak of events which were thought of as having worldwide repercussions, Christians – and Jesus himself – would turn naturally to an existing stock of images. Being what they are these images cannot provide information, and it would be silly to ask what precisely this or that detail was meant to refer to. They were not meant to refer to anything specific, only to build up a general picture of the crisis and conflict which would mark the end of *a* world and the beginning of another. If one is wondering about the End of *the* World, this page of Paul cannot be quoted, as extremists have done throughout history, as if it predicts exactly what is going to happen, because it doesn't.

The Coming of Christ: When?

Less still can it be quoted on the question of *when* it is going to happen, because it is clearly mistaken! True enough Paul's purpose of writing was to assure the community of Salonika that the Coming of Christ could not take place as soon as they were expecting. Nonetheless, his own expectations were not far behind theirs, for he saw the End coming as a climax of a struggle which had already reached its final stages. Logically and chronologically, Paul saw the Coming of Christ as the next item on the programme. This is clear enough from the excerpt just quoted, and no one in his senses would deny that if Paul were writing to Salonika today he would need to express himself rather differently.

In fact Paul did not have to wait 1900 years to change his mind. To the Salonikans he had written that at the Coming of Christ he expected, like them, still to be alive:

> Those who have died in Christ will be the first to rise, and then *those of us who are still alive* will be taken up in the clouds, together with them. (1 Thessalonians 4:17)

When he wrote to the Corinthians only five or six years later, he had already changed his tune and assumed that both he and they would already be dead:

> We know that he who raised the Lord Jesus to life *will raise us* with Jesus in our turn, and put us by his side, *and you with us.* (2 Corinthians 4:14)

In an attempt to save what is known as 'inerrancy' of scripture, there has been in the past much dishonesty over these texts of Paul. People thought it was their duty to tie themselves in knots to prove they were perfectly consistent with each other. In the interests of truth it would be far simpler to admit that in the first text Paul was in error about the date of Christ's Coming, and that the realisation of this later made him modify and deepen his views.

Barnaby's Picture Library

The word 'deepen' is important. Because, after all, what is most deeply significant about the Coming of Christ is not its date but its reality. Even if Paul speaks of it as if he had a telescope trained on the future, that is only his dramatic imagery. Underlying that imagery is the much more basic conviction that this future is really already upon us.

It is Paul's fundamental belief that in the life of Jesus of Nazareth, God has said all he wanted to say. In him the meaning of God has been exhausted. The Christ-event therefore, marks the ultimate turning point in history, and places all of us in the last days. From that time on, the Day of the Lord is no longer something to be waited for; it is an ever present reality as Christ comes into people's lives and faces them with the ultimate choices of life and death.

It is this deeper meaning of the Coming of Christ which is uppermost in Paul's later writings, where it is spoken of no longer as a single datable event in the future, but as a reality entering people's lives daily. Because Christ has died, and because Christ has risen, Christ comes again and again as people's ordinary lives are crossed by his, and challenged. The emphasis has shifted from the future to the present. In dramatic vein Paul may continue to represent the triumph of Christ as a future and ultimate one. But what he stresses is the fact that what is ultimately true is true here and now. It is not only the Last Day which is decisive, but every day.

It is this perspective, and the radical seriousness it gives to life, which ought finally to emerge from Paul's correspondence with Salonika. Anyone concentrating only on the chronological aspect of Christ's Coming would have to conclude that since Paul was quite simply mistaken on this topic, he has nothing to tell us today. But he has. He tells us of a nearness to Christ which is more than merely temporal, and of a yearning for that presence to become more and more palpable. He tells us of a life lived in the light of a constant coming of Christ, and of an unshakeable confidence in a 'heaven' which is not beyond history, but simply its deepest dimension. And Christians of today need that good news to be told to them no less than the first-century Christians of Salonika.

FOR DISCUSSION

1. There is a stark contrast between 1 and 2 Thessalonians on the subject of the future Coming of Christ. 1 Thessalonians presumes it is imminent. 2 Thessalonians suggests a long postponement. Later epistles of Paul quietly drop the subject. Two thousand years later, what should Christians think on this subject? What part does the Coming of Christ play in your life?

2. Paul's correspondence with the Christians of Salonika is marked with a note of gentle encouragement: 'You already know... I need only remind you... You are doing well, keep at it.' Find some excerpts from some official Church documents (Council decrees, Papal encyclicals, bishops' pastorals, or parish news letters) which echo this pastoral concern.

3. This chapter has suggested that Christian morality should be based on the great Christian dogmas – Trinity, Resurrection, Mystical Body, Parousia. On what basis do you do what you do, or avoid what you avoid?

4. Goings-on in Corinth (Corinthians)

Paul wrote his two letters to the Christians of Salonika about the year A.D. 50, while he was preaching at Corinth. The church he founded at Corinth gave him many more sleepless nights than Salonika had ever done, and five or six years later he had to enter into a fairly bulky correspondence with the Christians there.

Corinth

Corinth was a sort of red-light district of the ancient world. The term sounds a little facetious; in fact it is a rather tame one for a town which Renan described as 'one vast brothel'. And it was this because of its geographical position.

Corinth lies on the narrow neck of land connecting the Greek mainland with the Peloponnese peninsula. In that position it forms a bridge which has to be used not only by all north and southbound traffic, but by most of the sea-traffic coming from the east and west as well. The Corinth canal had not yet been dug, but all the shipping wishing to avoid the hazardous 200–mile journey round the Peloponnese would dock in either the eastern or western port of Corinth, and simply transfer its passengers and cargo across the four-mile isthmus to the other port. Smaller ships were even dragged overland bodily, on trolleys.

Corinth was therefore one of the busiest international ports in the ancient world, with a population of half a million, as cosmopolitan as could be found anywhere today. Frenchmen, Spaniards or Romans travelling east, and Palestinians, Syrians and Asians travelling west would all meet there. And to cater for their entertainment, Corinth provided a temple of Aphrodite, goddess of love, which was served by a thousand prostitutes. The Greeks, who had a word for everything, coined a new verb 'to corinthiate' which meant to live a dissolute life. And the Romans, no doubt surprised at the prices, added a new proverb to their collection: 'Few can afford a Corinthian holiday.'

Paul first made contact with Corinth about the year A.D. 50. He had come into Europe in response to the vision which pleaded with him to share with the west the gospel he had learned in the east, and in northern Greece had founded two Christian communities in Philippi and Salonika. But Jews intolerant of this message forced him to leave both places, and he eventually sought refuge in the south, in the university town of Athens. But even there he had only drawn a blank. As Luke told the story, his magnificent sermon on the Areopagus did no more than elicit polite laughter from the sophisticated crowds. And so, lonely and depressed, consumed with worry over the converts he had had to abandon in the north, and sick at heart over his failure in Athens, Paul moved to the last square on the Greek chessboard, Corinth. And Corinth was hardly the place to cheer the heart of a saint.

It is one of the New Testament's many surprising revelations that in this highly unlikely spot Paul founded one of the early church's most vigorous communities. It would seem to suggest that the Word of God is more likely to penetrate the frivolous than the sophisticated mind. With the Athenian intelligentsia he had simply lost out: there is no record that Athens ever produced any notable Christian community. Among the worldly Corinthians he established such a thriving church that it was renowned for cen-

Barnaby's Picture Library

turies after. Yet as many as two-thirds of the town's population were slaves, and Paul's prospective converts – as he was later to remind them – included 'profligates, idolaters, adulterers, homosexuals, thieves, usurers, drunkards, slanderers and swindlers... These are the sort of people some of you were once' (1 Corinthians 6:9–11). No wonder, he recalls in the same letter, even he had qualms about preaching the gospel to them:

When I came to you, it was not with any show of oratory or philosophy, but simply to tell you what God had guaranteed. During my stay with you, the only knowledge I claimed to have was about Jesus, and only about him as the crucified Christ. Far from relying on any power of my own, I came among you in great fear and trembling, and in my speeches and the sermons that I gave, there were none of the arguments that belong to philosophy; only a demonstration of the power of the Spirit. And I did this so that your faith should not depend on human philosophy but on the power of God (2:1–5).

Yet 'philosophy' was precisely what certain of Paul's rumbustious converts eagerly aspired to, as these pointed words make all too clear. The Corinthian correspondence is largely concerned with the problems raised by these intellectual pretensions.

Background

The trouble had started after Paul had left Corinth to look for new mission fields elsewhere. Paul, as we saw in the preceding chapter, was not the only missionary on the road at that time; there were plenty of them on circuit throughout the Middle East. Some were blatant charlatans, out for the profit there was to be made from preaching. But others in all sincerity saw it as their duty to undermine Paul's activity, either because as ardent Jews they objected to the way he was 'liberating' fellow Jews from the Law of Moses (we shall meet these later in the Galatian correspondence), or because as Christians they disagreed with Paul's interpretation of the gospel. This was the case with Corinth.

Their own interpretation of Christianity is known as a 'gnostic' one, because it made the human relationship with God a matter of 'gnosis' or knowledge. Christianity, for them, was a secret understanding of God, brought down from heaven by a pre-existent celestial Christ, who remained on earth in human disguise to reveal it to a closed circle of initiates, and then disappeared back into the world of God. Salvation consisted in getting in on this secret.

Now it is quite obvious that some of this gnostic imagery, unconsciously absorbed or deliberately adopted, has made its way into parts of the New Testament. But it is also obvious that the New Testament's main thrust is anti-gnostic. With their strong emphasis on a fully human Jesus, totally identified with a suffering humanity, teaching not a philosophical system of ideas for an élite but a way of life for all people, the New Testament writers agree in repudiating any thoroughgoing gnostic interpretation of the Christian message.

Yet a gnostic Christianity held a strong fascination for the first-century world, and not least in Corinth. A gospel which turned a blind eye on your behaviour as long as you had the right awareness or 'gnosis' (as a student of mine colourfully put it, 'the gnostic was allowed to fling a loose leg as long as he had his head screwed on') – this was very congenial to a highly permissive society. Further, the sophisticated Greek mind could not fail to be attracted to gnosticism's emphasis on the individual, its intellectual appeal and its flavour of élitism. The fact is that a Christianity of this type, palpably distinct from that which Paul had preached, invaded Corinth after Paul's departure, and split the small Christian community into factions. How deeply it had taken root is hard to say: certainly enough to worry Paul severely.

He had heard of the trouble when, a few years later, he had set off on another missionary journey and chosen Ephesus for his headquarters. Ephesus is only two hundred miles across the Aegean Sea from Corinth. Letters could pass to and fro in a

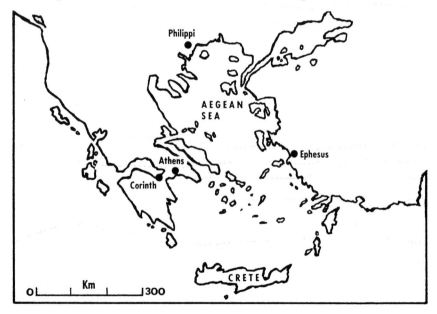

matter of days, and even personal visits could be made without much difficulty. Whether Paul actually visited Corinth from Ephesus, and how many letters passed between him and the community, is a matter of dispute. Of the correspondence, two of Paul's letters have survived in the New Testament.

The first is longer. Paul's aim is to sound out the situation and to assure himself of the loyalty of the young church before he can dare to tackle the 'Pseudo-Apostles,' as he later calls the rival missioners. At this stage he seems to be rather uncertain about them. The letter deals therefore simply with the abuses of which Paul has heard, and with the specific questions he has been asked to answer. It is only in retrospect that it is possible to see, between the lines, a number of veiled references to the rival preachers, about whom Paul is still feeling his way.

His strategy was well judged. The letter produced the desired effect of correcting the abuses in Corinth and eliciting a strong declaration of loyalty towards Paul. Within months he was back at his desk writing the second letter, to confirm the good relations he had re-established with the community, and to launch a frontal attack on the 'Pseudo-Apostles' with no holds barred. The year was A.D. 56 to 57.

Reading other people's letters is in many ways like listening in on one end of a telephone conversation. What is being said is clear enough. What precisely it means will depend on what is going on at the other end. And lacking that other half of the conversation, we can only reconstruct, that is to say, guess. In the case of the Corinthian correspondence, the guesswork of one scholar will not necessarily be the same as that of another. How many letters the correspondence consisted of, whether the present text represents two original letters or more, whether Paul visited Corinth in the course of the correspond-ence, and how many times – these are matters of interpreting the overtones and ambiguities of the letters. If one waited for final agreement on these fine details, one would never read the letters at all. Which would be a pity, because they are vintage Paul. We learn more of him from the letters to Corinth perhaps than from any other of his writings, of his passionate and stormy relationship with his converts, of his overwhelming desire to share with them his Christian insights, and of the depths from which those insights came.

Intellectualism (1 Corinthians 1–4)

The troubles in Corinth stemmed, as we have seen, from the fact that some of its Christians had pretensions to an intellectual type of Christianity. The extent to which Paul regards this as a perversion of the gospel may be gauged from the fact that he devotes the first four chapters of the correspondence to the matter. In fact he even adopts the technical terminology of gnosticism – the two letters are punctuated with the words 'revelation', 'hidden wisdom', 'philosophy', 'initiates', and even (25 times) the word 'gnosis' – to emphasise what the true knowledge of God really consists of. More pointedly still, the opening paragraph of the correspondence omits the usual prayer of thanksgiving for the faith, hope and love of his correspondents, and replaces it with fulsome praise of their 'gnosis.' The irony might best be conveyed with italics and exclamation marks:

> I give thanks to my God continually in your name for that grace of God which has been bestowed upon *you* in Jesus Christ; that you have become rich, through him, in every way, in *eloquence* and in *knowledge* of *every* sort, so *fully* has the message of Christ established itself among you! And now there is *no* gift in which you are still lacking! You have *only* to look forward to the revealing of our Lord Jesus Christ! (1 Corinthians 1:4–7, Knox version)

It is, of course, possible that Paul is not being so openly ironical. He mentions, a few verses later, that he is only going on what he has heard on the grapevine from below-stairs at Chloe's house, and these opening lines could be translated, 'I give thanks to my God for the perfection which, I am told, you have achieved...' Still, for a community which was reputed to find Paul's gospel rather pedestrian, and which aspired to a highly intellectualised Christianity, this first paragraph is distinctly chill. And yet Paul ends his prayer with utter sincerity and warmth. However frivolous the Corinthians may be, God is not:

> (God) *will* strengthen your resolution to the last, so that no charge will lie against you on the day when our Lord Jesus Christ comes. The God who has called you into the fellowship of his Son, Jesus Christ our Lord, is *faithful* to his promise. (1:8–9)

Eastern Daily Press

This mixture of severity and tenderness continues to characterise these opening pages. Paul is scathing about the sectarianism to which the new preaching has already led:

> I do appeal to you, brothers, for the sake of our Lord Jesus Christ, to make up the differences between you... What are all these slogans that you have, like 'I am for Paul', 'I am for Apollo', 'I am for Cephas', 'I am for Christ'? Has Christ been parcelled out? Was it Paul that was crucified for you? Were you baptised in the name of Paul? I am thankful that I never baptised any of you after Crispus and Gaius!... What could be more unspiritual than your slogans, 'I am for Paul' and 'I am for Apollo'! (1:10–14, 3:4)

He is enraged with anger at the though of anyone introducing these divisions among his converts:

> Didn't you realise that you were God's temple and that the Spirit of God was living among you? If anyone should destroy the temple of God, God will destroy him!... I will be visiting you soon... Do I come with a stick in my hand or in a spirit of love and goodwill? (3:16–17, 4:19–21)

He is blistering about the mental ability of the Corinthians to cope with anything really intellectual, anyway:

At the time when you were converted, how many of you were wise in the ordinary sense of the word, how many were influential people, or came from noble families?... Those whom the world thinks common and contemptible are the ones that God has chosen – those who are nothing at all!... What I fed you with was milk, not solid food, for you were not ready for it; and indeed you are still not ready for it!... If any one of you thinks of himself as wise, in the ordinary sense of the word, then he must learn to be a fool before he really can be wise. (1:26–28, 3:2,18)

He is adamant about keeping Christ's cross, and not any philosophical speculation, at the centre of Christianity:

Christ did not send me to baptise, but to preach the Good News, which is the crucifixion of Christ, and you cannot express that in terms of philosophy!... While the Greeks look for wisdom, here are we preaching a crucified Christ, which is to the pagans madness, but to those who have been called, a Christ who is the power and the wisdom of God... When I came to you, it was not with any show of oratory or philosophy... The only knowledge I claimed to have was about Jesus, and only about him as the crucified Christ. (1:17–2:2)

His concern for his converts is expressed, as it was in the letter's opening lines, in the bitterest of irony:

You, of course, already have everything you want! You are already rich, in possession of the Kingdom, with us left outside! Indeed I wish you were already in the Kingdom, so that we could share it with you! But instead, it seems to me, God has put us apostles at the end of his parade, with the men sentenced to death!... Here we are, fools for the sake of Christ, while you are the learned men in Christ! We have no power, but you are influential! You are celebrities, we are nobodies, the scum of the earth! (4:8–13)

But the irony soon turns, as it did earlier, to the tenderest of appeals:

I am saying all this not just to make you ashamed but to bring you, as my dearest children, to your senses. You might have thousands of guardians in Christ, but not more than one father! It was I who begot you in Christ Jesus by preaching

the Good News. That is why I beg you to copy me... and to
live the way that I live in Christ. (4:14–17)

What a signing-off line! It says much for the sincerity and
openness of Paul's relationship with his Christians that he can
propose himself, so simply and unselfconsciously, for their
imitation.

Sexual morality (1 Corinthians 5–6)

Once you have made your relationship with God an activity of
your mind ('gnosis'), then you have a choice about the attitude
you will take to the activity of your body. Either you will find
the body such an embarrassment that you crush it mercilessly.
Or you will regard it as so irrelevant to what really matters
that you give it free rein to do what it likes. With the first
attitude we are fairly familiar: a good deal of 'Christian'
asceticism has been purveyed in these terms. The second we
find more strange, yet it was a commonplace in the kind of
gnostic Christianity which had found its way into Corinth.

A Christian had attempted marriage with his step-mother.
Far from condeming this incestuous aberration, abhorrent to
Jewish and Roman law alike, the Corinthian intellectuals were
apparently quite happily condoning it. Their complacency
shocks Paul. Such shamelessness – and he means that of the
community as much as that of the sinner – is incompatible
with the new dimension of life to which the gospel has
introduced them. He demands that the offending Christian
shall be excommunicated forthwith, both for the sake of the
community which might otherwise be further infected, and for
his own sake: refusing to consort with him might bring him to
his senses:

> You should not associate with a brother Christian who is
> leading an immoral life, or is a usurer, or idolatrous, or a
> slanderer, or a drunkard, or is dishonest; you should not even
> eat a meal with people like that. (1 Corinthians 5:10–11)

The sentence sounds ferocious. Yet when his stern measures
are put into effect, Paul can be just as extreme in his
tenderness. A few months later we find him writing, apparently
on the same matter:

> I wrote as I did to make sure that, when I came, I should not
> be distressed by the very people who should have made me

happy. I am sure you all know that I could never be happy
unless you were... Someone has been the cause of pain not to
me, but to some degree – not to overstate it – to all of you.
The punishment already imposed by the majority on the
man in question is enough; and the best thing now is to give
him your forgiveness and encouragement, or he might break
down from so much misery. So I am asking you to give some
definite proof of your love for him... Anybody that you
forgive, I forgive. (2 Corinthians 2:3–10)

Not that the case of incest was the only instance in which
Paul's preaching was being undermined. There were some in
Corinth who claimed that their new Christian freedom justified
them in giving uninhibited expression to their sexual urges: it
was as natural as eating and drinking, and as little to do with
their relationship to God, which concerned the mind, not the
body. Paul refuses to have anything to do with this kind of
disembodied Christianity. And he bases his argument, as he
did with the Christians of Salonika, not simply on a law – he
agrees that for a Christian 'there are no *forbidden* things'
(1 Corinthians 6:12) – but on the deepest Christian realities.
   To begin with, the body is not be be explained simply in
terms of its needs and appetites. The Christian, at least, is
united to Christ, and so lives in terms of a body that will be
raised from the dead by the same *God* who raised Christ's:

'Food is only meant for the stomach and the stomach for
food.' Yes, and God is going to do away with both of them.
But the body – this is not meant for fornication; it is for the
Lord, and the Lord for the body. God, who raised the Lord
from the dead, will by his power raise us up too. (6:13–14)

In fact, he continues, the Christian's body is so closely
incorporated into Christ that to misuse that body would be to
misuse *Christ* himself:

You know, surely, that your bodies are members making up
the body of Christ; do you think that I can take parts of
Christ's body and join them to the body of a prostitute?
Never! (6:15)

To conclude, the Christian's incorporation into Christ has
made the body into the very temple of Christ's *Spirit*. To misuse
it is, in the last analysis, a kind of sacrilege:

Your body, you know, is the temple of the Holy Spirit, who is in you since you received him from God. You are not your own property. (6:19)

In short, the body is not to be regarded as irrelevant, less still as a barrier standing between the true self and God. In Paul's theology (and in this he is true to the deepest insights of the Old Testament), people do not simply and regrettably *have* bodies; they *are* bodies, and it is in and through their very bodiliness that they must 'glorify God', that is to say, bring about the very presence of God in the world. (6:20)

Answers to problems (1 Corinthians 7–11)

In a third section of this letter, Paul turns away from the abuses, of which he knows only by hearsay, to the questions which the Corinthians had specifically put to him. And because he has been dealing with sexual morality, he takes first the questions they had asked about marriage.

Some people's reading of Paul has never got any further than 1 Corinthians 7, and from its tone they conclude that he must have been a misogynist. But it is unfair to judge him on this chapter alone, because here he is answering some very twisted questions, and his answers necessarily reflect that fact. The Corinthians, here in their more rigorist mood, had asked whether marriage partners, now that they had become Christians, should stop sleeping together. Or perhaps even break up the marriage altogether? At least in the case where one of the partners had not become a Christian? Should widows or widowers regard themselves as providentially liberated from bodily tyranny, from which it would be madness to turn to a second marriage? Should not young people stay single, especially in view of a Coming of Christ which might take place at any moment? What of engaged couples – should they break off their engagement for the same reason?

The questions are so bizarre that it is surprising to find Paul coming up with such sensible answers.

Those who are widowed or engaged to be married, he insists, must be left entirely free. Their choice is a matter of vocation, not morality.

As for those already married, whether to fellow Christians or not, they are not to dream of separating. As the gospel makes clear, they have committed themselves and have not the same freedom of choice. And because of that commitment, they have

Barnaby's Picture Library

obligations which they cannot shrug off on pseudo-spiritual grounds:

> The husband must give his wife what she has the right to expect, and so too the wife to the husband. The wife has no rights over her own body; it is the husband who has them. In the same way, the husband has no rights over his body; the wife has them. Do not refuse each other except by mutual consent, and then only for an agreed time, to leave yourselves free for prayer; then come together again in case Satan should take advantage of your weakness to tempt you.
> (1 Corinthians 7:3–5)

No concessions to gnostic asceticism here.

On the question of celibacy he cannot be so unbiassed. It is his own chosen way of life, and throughout the chapter he makes no bones about his prejudice:

> Yes, it is a good thing for a man not to touch a woman. (v.1)
> I should like everyone to be like me. (v.7)
> It is a good thing for the unmarried to stay as they are, like me. (v.9)
> If you are free of a wife, then do not look for one. (v.27)
> The man who marries his partner does a good thing but the man who does not marry her does something even better. (v.38)
> A widow would be happier, in my opinion, if she stayed as she is. (v.40)

The grounds on which he bases this opinion are, at first sight, surprising:

In these present times of *stress*... married people will suffer
grief in their lives... Brothers, this is what I mean: our *time* is
growing *short*. Those who have wives should live as though
they had none, and those who mourn should live as though
they had nothing to mourn for; those who are enjoying life
should live as though there were nothing to laugh about;
those whose life is buying things should live as though they
had nothing of their own; and those who have to deal with
the world should not become engrossed with it. I say this
because the world as we know it is *passing away*.

I would like to see you free from all *worry*. An unmarried
man can devote himself to the Lord's affairs, all he need
worry about is pleasing the Lord; but a married man has to
bother about the world's affairs and devote himself to pleasing
his wife: he is torn two ways... I say this only to help you, not
to put a halter round your necks, but simply to make sure...
that you give your undivided attention to the Lord. (7:26–35)

The words italicised in the text are the technical ones used
elsewhere in the New Testament about the End of the World.
That being the case, it would seem at first sight that Paul's
advice is rather misplaced. If he was so wrong on the date of
the Coming of Christ, what possible value can there be in his
recommendation of celibacy?

But as we have seen in the correspondence with Salonika,
Paul's advice is not based on the date of Christ's Coming, but
on its significance. Paul is not arguing on mere chronology, but
on the fact that in the Christ-event history, in one sense, has
come to an end. Everyone since Christ is living in the 'last
times'. The world as it once was is in the process of
disappearing, and a new era has begun, of which the previous
world can only be a shadow. To be engrossed in that world,
whether socially, economically or emotionally, should no
longer be possible for a Christian committed to seeing it only
as the chrysalis out of which the new Kingdom of God is
emerging.

Christians therefore ought to show a certain detachment
from the world as they once knew it. Celibates are able to bear
dramatic witness to this dimension of Christianity, in the way
married people are not free to do. The presumption, of course
(as will be pointed out in the letter to the Ephesians), is that
they recognise the witness to other dimensions given by their
non-celibate brothers and sisters.

Two further problems occupy Paul's attention in this section of the letter. Neither of them is particularly relevant to the world we live in today: whether one may eat meat left over from temple-sacrifices which has made its way back to the butcher, and whether women should wear hats in church. But what is of far greater interest here than the detailed answers Paul gives to these cases of conscience is the delicacy, courtesy and charity with which he solves the problems presented to him. Determined to be all things to all men, and writing as he is to a town which hosted the famous Isthmian Games every two years, he is in one and the same sentence a runner training for a track event, a boxer dieting to reduce his weight, an announcer calling out the names in the stadium, and an athlete hoping he has not been disqualified! (9:26–27).

Yet it is not on mere wordplay that he finally bases his advice; it is, as always, on the deepest Christian realities. Corinthian scruples about what may or may not be eaten are to be solved by reflecting on the meaning of Christ's sacrificial death, of the social dimensions of the eucharist, of the unity of the church as the body of Christ, and above all of the charity without which that body must disintegrate:

> If food could be the occasion of my brother's downfall, I would never eat meat again in case I was the cause of a brother's downfall. (8:13)

It must, however, be admitted that even Paul gets out of his depth on the subject of appropriate headgear for church meetings. He toys with the idea that female hair is already a kind of veil – nature's own indication that women's heads should be covered. He appeals to the fact that the very angels cover their heads in awe before God – but this rather spoils his case for men remaining uncovered. He wonders whether bareheadedness is a surreptitious bid for equality with men, when everybody knows that woman was created out of man – but he has to add lamely that no one can deny that all men are born out of women! In final desperation he can only appeal to conformity:

> To anyone who might still want to argue: it is not the custom with us, nor in the churches of God. (11:16)

He could not bear the thought of people regarding the Corinthian church as an oddity.

Individualism (1 Corinthians 11–14)

The problems of hats in church has raised the larger question of decorum in public worship, and Paul turns to two related areas, both bedevilled by the individualism to which previous problems had shown the Corinthians to be prone.

The eucharist, in the earliest times, was celebrated in the context of an 'agape' meal: food which had been brought along by the participants was shared around as an expression of brotherliness and unity. The trouble at Corinth, with its lack of a sense of community, was that the sharing was non-existent.

The docker with his cheese sandwiches sat in one corner, the magnate with his caviare in another. Some were even bringing so much liquor with them that they were under the table before the eucharist proper started.

Paul's tone is one of subdued anger:

Barnaby's Picture Library

I hear that when you all come together as a community, there are separate factions among you, and I half believe it – since there must no doubt be separate groups among you, to distinguish those who are important! The point is, when you held these meetings, it is not the *Lord's* supper that you are eating, since when the time comes to eat, everyone is in such a hurry to start his *own* supper that one person goes hungry while another is getting drunk. Surely you have homes for eating and drinking in? Surely you have enough respect for the community of God not to make poor people embarrassed? What am I to say to you? Congratulate you?...

This is what I received from the Lord, and in turn passed on to you: that on the same night that he was betrayed, the Lord Jesus took some bread, and thanked God for it and broke it, and he said, 'This is my body, which is for you; do *this* as a memorial of me.' In the same way he took the cup after supper, and said, 'This cup is the new covenant in my blood. Whenever you drink it, do *this* (and not anything else) as a memorial of me.' Until the Lord comes, therefore, every time you eat this bread and drink this cup, you are proclaiming his death...

Everyone is to recollect himself before eating this bread and drinking this cup... When you meet for the Meal, wait for one another. Anyone who is hungry should eat at home... The other matters I shall adjust when I come.
(1 Corinthians 11:18–34)

It is again noteworthy how Paul solves his problems by appealing not to canon law but to the most basic Christian realities. His decisions are totally practical, but they are based on the deepest of motives. There must be an end of cliques, selfishness and dissipation, not because they are 'forbidden', but simply because the eucharist is a common sharing of the one Christ, a re-presentation of Christ's own charity, and a re-enactment of Christ's own death.

His advice on 'charismata' (chapters 12–14) is less concise. The word means '(spiritual) gifts', and refers to the various activities or roles, ordinary as well as extraordinary, in which the life of the church manifests itself. The Corinthians, with their gnostic and individualist leanings, had put a premium on the more exotic of these roles, and in their disregard of others while exercising them, had reduced religious assemblies to a literal pandemonium, where every 'daemon' or spirit was given free rein. Inspired 'prophets' vied with those claiming to speak in 'tongues', and ecstatics with miracle-workers.

Paul has to tread warily here. He is aware that in no area of their lives are people more susceptible to self-deception than in 'gifts' of this kind. So he certainly cannot be all approval. But neither can be he all disapproval: to bear down too heavily on this matter could quench the Spirit altogether.

He begins by emphasising the gratuitous character of all charisms. If every talent, endowment or role in the church is an unearned gift, how can anyone preen himself on possessing one rather than another? Worse still, how can anyone use her particular gift to bring about disunity, and so obscure the one bountiful source from which they all come?

There is a variety of gifts but always the same Spirit... One may have the gift of preaching given by the Spirit; another may have the gift of teaching given by the same Spirit; and another the gift of faith given by the same Spirit; another the gift of healing, through this one Spirit; one, the power of miracles; another, prophetic powers; another the gift of distinguishing spiritual gifts; another the gift of 'tongues' and another the ability to interpret them. All these are the work of one and the same Spirit, who distributes different gifts to different people just as he chooses. (12:4–11)

The list is as haphazard as the untidy life of the church. Nor are all the gifts mentioned extraordinary ones; the quite ordinary roles of preaching and teaching are mentioned here, and when Paul gives other random lists elsewhere he includes administration, missionary work, poverty relief work, and even marriage – all of them are charisms. In fact it is significant that in this first list, the more exotic gifts so prized at Corinth are left to the end.

For in Paul's mind, charisms are nothing other than the roles exercised by various members of a Spirit-filled church, enabling it to function as a community. He compares the community to a human body, where the unseen roles are often more vital than the ostentatious ones. But the word 'compares' is too weak: the church *is* a body, the very resurrection-body through which the risen Christ continues to express himself in the world:

Just as a human body, though it is made up of many parts, is a single unit because all these parts, though many, make up one body, so it is with *Christ*... The body is not to be identified with any one of its many parts... If your whole body was just one eye, how would you hear anything? If it was just one ear, how would you smell anything?... If all the parts were the same, how could it be a body? As it is, the parts are many but the body is one. The eye cannot say to the hand, 'I do not need you', nor can the head say to the feet, 'I do not need you.'

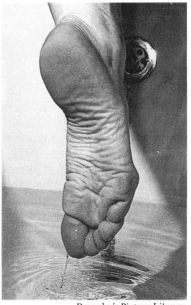

Barnaby's Picture Library

What is more, it is precisely the parts of the body that seem to be the weakest which are the indispensable ones: and it is the least honourable parts of the body that we clothe with the greatest care. God has arranged the body so that... there may not be disagreements inside the body, but that each part may be equally concerned for all the others. If one part is hurt, all parts are hurt with it. If one part is given special honour, all parts enjoy it.

Now you together *are* Christ's body. (12:12–27)

And in such a body, the most fundamental 'function', without which the whole organism must come to a standstill, is charity. This, too, Paul calls a 'charism', in fact the best of all. In all their concentration on intellectual gifts, the Corinthians have overlooked the most precious gift God has to bestow on the human race, love.

It has been pointed out that in this most well-known passage of Scripture, where Paul describes the kind of love he has in mind ('charity is patient, is kind...'), he is really pointing a portrait for which Jesus sat. The text might more appropriately be translated as follows:

> He was never in a hurry
>   and was always kindness itself.
> He never envied anybody at all
>   and never boasted about himself.
> He was never snobbish
>   or rude, or selfish.
> He didn't keep on talking
>   about the wrong things other people do;
>   remembering the good things
>   was happiness enough for him.
> He was tough –
>   he could face anything.
> And he never lost trust in God,
>   or in men and women.
> He never lost hope.
> And he never gave in. (13:4–7, A.T.Dale's translation)

If Christians are not Christlike, then all their other qualifications, however brilliant, are worth no more than the banging of a tin can.

It used to be the fashion to depict the early church as a community of freewheeling 'charismatics', which was only later regrettably transformed into the rigidly hierarchical society with which people have become familiar ever since. Those commentaries which speak of charisms as if they were special gifts bestowed upon a few in order to 'help the church to function while its hierarchy was still in a rudimentary state' (Jerusalem Bible *ad loc.*) compound this strange error. Certainly Paul makes no such distinction between charismatics and hierarchs. It is true that the eccentrics of Corinth are given more than their fair share of the limelight in these chapters. It is also clear that Paul, willing as he is to acknowledge the possibility of a genuine God-given gift of 'tongues', is more than half suspicious that the phenomena at Corinth are delusory and self-induced: in what he says about them here he could hardly have been more discouraging. But what emerges most forcibly from these pages is his conviction that a role in the church does not have to be extraordinary before it can be classified a charism. The most ordinary task of teaching requires its charism as much as the more flamboyant gift of 'tongues' or ecstatic utterances. The administrator is no less 'chosen' by God than the prophet, and each must pay due heed to the other if the risen body of Christ is to live on in the world.

Intellectualism again (1 Corinthians 15)

Paul has left until the last the trickiest of the questions on which his Corinthian correspondents required further advice, the resurrection of the dead. Their difficulties with this tenet of the Christian faith seem to have been rooted in the same intellectualism which, as we have seen, gave rise to the problems of chapters 1–4. The letter therefore ends on the note on which it began.

Anyone who sees religion in intellectual terms, where relationship with God is expressed in terms of knowledge and understanding, will tend to live in hopes of the survival of the intellectual or spiritual part of him – the soul. That salvation could concern that prison of the soul which we call the body is almost unthinkable. The Greeks thought along these lines, and found Paul's preaching of a resurrection of the body so extraordinary when he first proposed it to them at Athens that they exploded with laughter (Acts 17:32).

Neither the Old Testament, nor the gospel which is heir to its thought, made this sharp dichotomy between body and soul. There the hope is for the salvation of the whole person, who is not thought of as a soul temporarily caged in a body, but as a body marvellously endowed, unlike other bodies, with the power of thinking and loving. For both the Old and the New Testament, unless people survived as *bodies* they could not be said to survive at all.

Whether the Corinthians with their Greek background had never really grasped this in the first place, or whether their flirtation with gnosticism had made them revert to a Greek way of thinking, the fact is that Paul finds it necessary to go to considerable lengths to underline the importance of bodily resurrection in the Christian scheme of things.

And first, the resurrection of Christ, which stands at the very centre of the good news proclaimed by Christianity. If, as Greek philosophy maintained, bodily resurrection is simply out of the question, then:

> Christ himself cannot have been raised. And if Christ has not been raised then our preaching is useless and your believing it is useless; indeed, we are shown up as witnesses who have committed perjury before God, because we swore in evidence before God that he *had* raised Christ to life. For if the dead are not raised, Christ has not been raised, and if Christ has not been raised, you are still in your sins...
> (1 Corinthians 15:14–18)

even though he had died a thousand times 'for men's sins'. For the resurrection of Christ is not a mere apologetic proof of the truth of his teaching, it is the very means by which people are united with God. The Christian message is not of a Christ who once revealed a philosophy of life and has now disappeared. It is of a Christ who lives on, beyond death, in and through his followers.

Christ's resurrection is therefore central to the Christian message. But so also is the resurrection of every Christian. If Christ rose from the dead, his followers cannot *not* rise from the dead. Incorporated into him, they are now the very resurrection-body of Christ, the beginning of a new human race. The risen Christ was but the first sheaf of a harvest, which cannot be taken up unless the rest of the harvest is ready for reaping likewise:

> But Christ *has* in fact been raised from the dead, the first-fruits of all who have fallen asleep. Death came through one man and in the same way the resurrection of the dead

Eastern Daily Press

has come through one man. Just as all men die in Adam, so all men will be brought to life in Christ. (15:20–3)

What resurrection consists of, Paul finds it harder to express, for he has as little information on this mystery as anyone else. What he can do is recall the image used by Jesus himself, of the seed that must die in its solitariness before it can be transformed into a harvest:

Whatever you sow in the ground
has to die before it is given new life
and the thing that you sow
is not what is going to come...
The thing that is sown is perishable
but what is raised is imperishable;
the thing that is sown is contemptible
but what is raised is glorious;
the thing that is sown is weak
but what is raised is powerful;
when it is sown it embodies the soul,
when it is raised it embodies the spirit.
If the soul has its own embodiment,
so does the spirit have its own embodiment...
Flesh and blood cannot inherit the kingdom of God:
and the perishable cannot inherit what lasts for ever.
(15:36–50)

The analogy has its shortcomings, but at least it warns us against understanding resurrection in too crassly materialistic a way, as if it had to do with bringing back to life the 'flesh and blood' which make up the physical body. Flesh and blood do not inherit the kingdom of God, either before death or after. In order to be 'with God', the body as we now know it must be transformed. Like the crucified body of Jesus, it must enter into a new mode of existence. Christians must be able to describe their own life as they describe Christ's risen life, as an embodied sharing of themselves with others. Insofar as people have already experienced this, the resurrection of the body can be said to have begun. Indeed in future letters, beginning with 2 Corinthians, Paul does not hesitate to speak of the Christian's resurrection as a present reality, and not only a future one.

2 Corinthians

Paul's second letter to Corinth cannot be analysed as closely as the first. To begin with, it is far more allusive and obscure, with more than usually large amounts of the 'telephone conversation' taking place outside the text. The drift of this can only vaguely be guessed at. But Paul himself is also far less coherent here. This is no orderly treatment of problems that have been put before him. It is a rambling personal apologia.

Paul is in the dock. His authority has been questioned and his character attacked. He must defend his good name and re-establish his authority even at the cost of digressing. One digression leads him a dance through four and a half chapters (2 Corinthians 2:14 – 7:4) before he returns to the point in question.

Yet it is in these digressions that his writing is at its best. He may only be defending himself against the charges of insincerity levelled against him, but the illustrations he uses to throw light on his argument are pure gospel. Some of the best known and frequently quoted words of Paul come from this letter:

> Blessed be the God and Father of our Lord Jesus Christ, a gentle Father and the God of all consolations, who comforts us in all our sorrows. (2 Corinthians 1:3–4)

> Thanks be to God who, wherever he goes, makes us, in Christ, partners of his triumph, and through us is spreading the knowledge of himself, like a sweet smell, everywhere. We are Christ's incense to God. (2:14–15)

Where the Spirit of the Lord is, there is freedom. (3:17)

We, with our unveiled faces reflecting like mirrors the glory of the Lord, all grow brighter and brighter as we are turned into the image that we reflect. (3:18)

It is the same God that said, 'Let there be light shining out of darkness', who has shone in our minds to radiate the knowledge of God's glory, the glory on the face of Christ. (4:6)

Always, wherever we may be, we carry with us in our body the death of Jesus, so that the life of Jesus, too, may always be seen in our body... There is no weakening on our part, and instead, though this outer man of ours may be falling into decay, the inner man is renewed day by day. Yes, the troubles which are soon over, though they weigh little, train us for the carrying of a weight of eternal glory which is out of all proportion to them. (4:10–17)

The love of Christ overwhelms us... If one man has died for all, then all men should be dead; and the reason he died for all was so that living men should live no longer for themselves, but for him who died and was raised to life for them. (5:14–15)

Even if we did once know Christ in the flesh, that is not how we know him now. And for anyone who is in Christ, there is a new creation; the old creation has gone, and now the new one is here. (5:16–17)

God in Christ was reconciling the world to himself, not holding men's faults against them, and he has entrusted to us the good news that they are reconciled. (5:19)

For our sake God made the sinless one into sin, so that in him we might become the goodness of God. (5:21)

Remember how generous the Lord Jesus was: he was rich, but he became poor for your sake, to make you rich out of his poverty. (8:9)

The jealousy that I feel for you is God's own jealousy: I arranged for you to marry Christ so that I might give you away as a chaste virgin to this one husband. (11:2)

The grace of the Lord Jesus Christ, the love of God and the fellowship of the Holy Spirit be with you all. (13:13)

Paul and the Corinthians

These texts shine out like jewels. Yet, it must be repeated, they are in fact only incidental to Paul's main purpose in writing this letter. They are no more than splendid asides, as it were, on his principal theme – the re-establishment of good relations with his correspondents, before he can hope to launch an all-out attack on the disturbers of their peace. How angry that attack eventually was we have already seen in the excerpt quoted above pp. 8 – 11. But that anger was inspired by a genuine love and a desperate anxiety for his converts, as the following passages from his main theme movingly witness:

> You must all join in prayers for me: the more people there are asking for help for me, the more will be giving thanks when it is granted to me. (2 Corinthians 1:11)

> I have always treated everybody, and especially you, with the reverence and sincerity which come from God. (1:12)

> There are no hidden meanings in my letters besides what you can read for yourselves and understand. (1:13)

> I hope that... you can be as proud of me as I am of you. (1:14)

Barnaby's Picture Library

Do you really think... that I say Yes, yes, and No, no at the same time? (1:17)

I am not a dictator over your faith. (1:24)

At least I do not go round offering the word of God for sale, as many other people do. (2:17)

Unlike other people, I need no letters of recommendation either to you or from you, because you are yourselves my letter, written in my heart, that anybody can see and read, and it is plain that you are a letter from Christ. (3:1–3)

It is not myself that I am preaching, but Christ Jesus as the Lord, and myself as your servant for Jesus' sake. (4:5)

I am only the earthenware jar that holds this treasure. (4:7)

I see no answer to my problems, but never despair. (4:8)

If I seemed out of my senses, it was for God; but if I am being reasonable now, it is for your sake. (5:13)

I am said to be dying, yet here I am alive; rumoured to be executed before I am sentenced; thought to be most miserable and yet I am always rejoicing; taken for a pauper although I make other people rich. (6:9–10)

Corinthians, I have spoken to you very frankly; my mind has been opened in front of you. Any constraint that you feel is not on my side; the constraint is in your own selves. I speak as if to children of mine: as a fair exchange, open your minds in the same way. (6:11–13)

Keep a place for me in your hearts. I have not injured anyone, or ruined anyone, or exploited anyone. I am not saying this to put any blame on you; as I have already told you, you are in my heart – together we live or together we die. (7:2–3)

To tell you the truth, even if I distressed you by my letter, I do not regret it... because your suffering led to your repentance. Yours has been a kind of suffering that God approves, and so you have come to no kind of harm from us. Just look at what suffering in God's way has brought you: what keenness, what explanations, what indignation, what alarm! Yes, and what aching to see me, what concern for me, and what justice done! (7:8–11)

In front of all the churches, give them a proof of your love, and prove to them that I was right to be proud of you. (8:24)

I pray to God that you will do nothing wrong: not that I want to appear as the one who has been successful – I would rather that you did well even though I failed. (13:7)

Few writings still valued for their theological content throb with life as these pages do; theology was not always academic and dull. Few letters from Christian leaders to their people have been as theologically rich as these, or as refreshingly open: pastoral letters were not always theologically thin and impersonal. It was Paul's genius to combine a mind of extraordinary depth with a personality that was unashamedly human, and none of his writings illustrate this better than the correspondence with Corinth.

It may be thought that this correspondence can have little relevance for Christians today, whose problems, great as they may be, are hardly those of the Corinthians. There is some truth in this: it would be difficult to find a place for the frenetic Corinthian community within the recognised structures of a modern diocese in the western world. On the other hand, the energy and optimism with which Paul threw himself into the task of preaching the gospel to them, convinced that even out of this chaos a people of God could be created (Acts 18:9–10), should give pause for thought to those who claim that some situations are simply too intractable for evangelisation.

Nor should it be too easily assumed that the gnostic perversion of Christianity, with which this correspondence is so concerned, is by now a dead letter. Indeed, good gnostic sermons are preached each Sunday from many pulpits, where God and Christ are presented as living in a world unbridgeably remote from the world of human beings, where the divinity of Christ is so spoken of that it effectively denies his brotherhood with the rest of the human race, where his fleeting 'visit' among us was for the purpose of revealing to an élite a set of truths otherwise unknown to the world, and where right relationship with God consists of escaping from the body as he did, in order to preserve those heavenly truths.

To people exposed to a 'Christianity' of this sort, Paul's message must still sound like the good news that it is: that God has never been absent from our world, which he lovingly accepts even before it 'repents', and that the life of Jesus of Nazareth was simply the supreme illustration of the fact that he is to be found in something as ordinary as the life of a man, who continues his human existence among his fellow human beings by being embodied in them.

There is no reason why such good news should not once again gladden the hearts (and bodies) of people and rescue them from the gloomy sectarianism into which they so easily relapse without it.

FOR DISCUSSION

1. At Corinth, Paul found that the gospel he preached made the greatest initial appeal not to intellectuals but to the dregs of society (see pp.38 and 39). Is this a commendation of Christianity or a criticism?

2. Paul's complaint is that the Corinthian church had over-intellectualised the gospel. What complaint would you make about your church?

3. Paul compares the Christian life to an incense, spreading the sweet smell of Christ through the world. To what extent do you think the history of the Church bears him out? Or the history of your life?

5. Thank You, Lydia and Co. (Philippians)

A chance remark make by Paul in the middle of his trouble-some correspondence with Corinth indicates that he had his own problems while he was writing from Ephesus:

> The things I had to undergo in Asia were more of a burden than I could carry, so that I despaired of coming through alive. Yes, I was carrying my own death warrant with me. (2 Corinthians 1:8–9)

The language suggests either a severe illness or an imprison-ment with a threatened death sentence. The letter to the Christians of Philippi contains over a dozen references to the

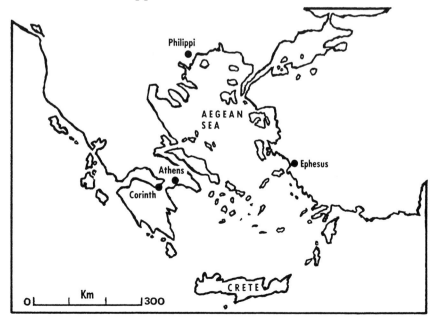

fact that it is written from prison, and that Paul is aware that he may not leave it alive. Many scholars today conclude that it was written, not from the Roman prison at the end of Paul's life as was once assumed, but from Ephesus, at about the same time that the Corinthian letters were being written, A.D. 56 to 57. The letter speaks of the frequent contact which the Philippians had established with Paul's prison. This would be understandable at Ephesus down the coast, less so overseas at Rome.

Philippi

The Philippians were Paul's first European converts. He had ventured into northern Greece from Asia Minor in response to his vision of a west as anxious to receive the gospel as the east, and Philippi was the first stop on his itinerary. The more prominent towns of Salonika, Athens and Corinth only came later, in second place.

Whether or not this created a special corner for the Philippians in Paul's heart, the fact is that he treated them differently from any of his other communities. Charged with money-grubbing, he had made it a rule in his missionary journeys to support himself by his own manual labour, and to accept no lecture fees from his converts. From the Philippians he accepted not only hospitality (a particularly persistent lady called Lydia is mentioned in Acts 16:15 and 40 as brooking no refusal) but also the considerable subsidy which allowed him to continue his mission through the rest of Greece. Indeed, the only way Paul later seems to be able to move the more parsimonious southerners to support his Jerusalem Relief Fund is to keep on reminding them of the generosity of these northerners – 'the Macedonians'. He seems to have felt more at ease with the Philippians, and less vulnerable, than with any other group of people. He can be open with them, and trust them, to a degree that this most open of human beings cannot allow himself elsewhere.

On a subsequent missionary journey, Paul has made his headquarters at Ephesus. During his three-year programme there, his preaching arouses the kind of violent opposition instanced in the riot of Acts 19:23, and Paul finds himself imprisoned. Three hundred miles up the coast, the news reaches Philippi, and a Paul Relief Fund is set up, organised no doubt by the irresistible Lydia. It is the arrival of this unsolicited gift that inspires Paul to write his epistle to the Philippians, primarily as a thank you letter:

> It was good of you to share with me in my hardships. In the early days of the Good News, as you people of Philippi well know, when I left Macedonia, no other church helped me with gifts of money. You were the only ones; and twice since my stay in Thessalonica you have sent me what I needed. It is not your gift that I value; what is valuable to me is the interest that is mounting up in your account. Now for the time being I have everything that I need and more: I am fully provided now that I have received... the offering that you sent, a sweet fragrance – the sacrifice that God accepts and finds pleasing. In return my God will fulfil all your needs, in Christ Jesus, as lavishly as only God can. (4:14–19)

Joy and Love

Surprisingly, given the circumstances in which it was written, the letter is full of joy. The word occurs in the text of this short letter as many as sixteen times, giving it a radiance unlike that of any other of Paul's letters. This refrain-like quality is obscured by the standard translations of the New Testament, where literary requirements are thought to rule out the repeated use of the same word. But what Paul actually says is (my translation):

> Every time I pray for all of you, I pray with *joy*.
> (Philippians 1:4)

> Christ is proclaimed, and that gives me *joy*; I shall continue to *rejoice*. (1:18–19)

> I feel sure I shall survive... to add *joy* to your faith. (1:25)

> Be united... that is the one thing which would fill me with *joy*. (2:2)

> If my blood has to be shed... I shall still *rejoice* and share my *joy* with you, and you must *rejoice* too, and let me share your *joy*. (2:17–18)

> You will *rejoice* to see him (Paul's postman) again... Give him a most *joyful* welcome in the Lord. (2:28–9)

> Finally, my brothers, *rejoice* in the Lord. It is no trouble to me to repeat what I have already written to you. (3:1)

I miss you very much, dear friends; you are my *joy*. (4:1)

I want you to *rejoice* always, in the Lord; I repeat, what I want is your *joy*. (4:4)

It is a great *joy* to me, in the Lord, that you have again shown concern for me. (4:10)

To bubble over with such joy when you are on Death Row is, to say the least, unusual. Presumably Paul feels the need to keep up the spirits of his anxious correspondents. But there is clearly no play-acting about his joy. His knowledge of Christ has given him a relationship with God so overwhelming that, here at least, the mere question of life and death fades out of the picture:

My one hope and trust is that... Christ will be glorified in my body, whether by my life or by my death. Life to me, of course, is Christ, but then death would bring me something more... I do not know what I should choose. (1:20–22)

One could speak of Christian resignation and detachment, except that the words have too cold a ring about them. Paul's joy is so genuinely warm that he can afford to turn even his jail into a joke: the gospel is being preached now to people who would not otherwise have heard of it:

I am glad to tell you, brothers, that the things that happened to me have actually been a help to the Good News. My chains in Christ, have become famous not only all over Government House but everywhere. (1:12–13)

It is almost as if the guards were chained to Paul, rather than he to them!

Paul's joy, and his concern to share it with his correspondents, is linked in this letter with a strong emphasis on love and unity. He presumes that nothing is so destructive of genuine joy as self-importance and lack of consideration for others. There is no kill-joy like the egotist. So he makes unity and love the subject of his opening prayer for them:

God knows how much I miss you all, loving you as Christ Jesus loves you. My prayer is that your love for each other increase more and more (1:8–9).

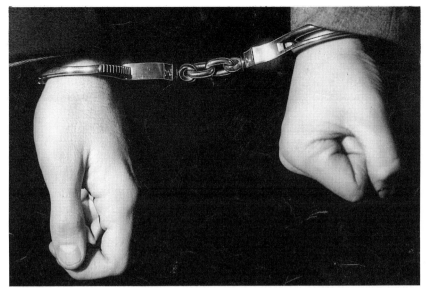

Barnaby's Picture Library

This subject remains central to the main body of advice in the letter:

> Avoid anything in your everyday lives that would be unworthy of the gospel of Christ, so that... you are unanimous in meeting the attack... united by your love... If our life in Christ means anything to you, if love can persuade at all... then be united in your convictions and united in your love... There must be no competition among you, no conceit; but everybody is to be self-effacing. Always consider the other person to be better than yourself, so that nobody thinks of his own interests first but everybody thinks of other people's interests instead. (1:27 – 2:5).

And in his closing remarks, Paul is still on the same subject:

> So then, my brothers and dear friends, do not give way... You are my joy and my crown. I appeal to Evodia and I appeal to Synteche to come to agreement with each other, in the Lord; and I ask you, Syzygus, to be true to your name and be a 'companion' to help them in this. (4:1–3)

Paul's tone in these passages is markedly less urgent than it was in his correspondence with Corinth. Private squabbling is not in the same class as open schism in the community.

Nonethless Paul cannot treat it as of no consequence. One is as erosive as the other, not only of the life of the community (and in Philippi this mattered: they, unlike the Corinthians, were living under persecution), but of the individuals involved. It destroys in them the image of Christ. They no longer portray, as the whole Christian vocation demands they should, the Man for Others.

It is typical of Paul that he should turn so naturally to theology to back up his moral advice. I have pointed out how frequently he does this throughout his letters. Here he does it to perfection. Parish feuds are out not because that is the law, or because discord is less noble than concord, or because trespassers will be prosecuted – but simply because they do not express the Christian reality. They are incompatible with Jesus' death and resurrection. If Evodia, Synteche and Syzygus are at loggerheads (or, as it might be, Evelyn, Sylvia and Sydney), then theology is not a speculative irrelevance but the most practical of truths. Paul could have given us no clearer insight into his mind than on this page, where he produces the New Testament's most priceless christological text – as a parenthesis on bickering in the Mothers' Union:

Barnaby's Picture Library

You must face life as Jesus did:

Like Adam, he was the image of God;
but unlike Adam, did not presume
that being like God meant to domineer.

He knew it meant to renounce all claims,
except the claim to be servant of all.

So he lived the life of a human being,
and accepted the human fate, which is death,
even the shameful death of a slave.

That is why God has raised him up,
and given him a title beyond compare:

Every creature, living and dead,
will kneel to him, and give glory to God,
and echo the cry, 'Jesus is Lord.'
(2:5–11, author's translation)

The translation tries to bring out not only the rhythmical pattern of this passage (so marked that many think Paul is quoting an existing hymn rather than here and now composing one), but also its meaning. Jesus, the Man for Others, is presented as the antithesis of Adam, the Man for Himself. Both created in the image of God, one tried to exploit that prerogative for his own advantage, the other more truly showed whose son he was by his humility. By hiding his glory, he gave himself away, as God does. The extent of his self-emptying must be judged from the fact that he was willing to die as slaves died – as even Paul the Roman citizen could not be forced to die.

In him, therefore, Paul sees as in an undistorting mirror what God is really like, and understands the God who is otherwise a total mystery. No one who has recognised Jesus for what he is can deny him the name which the Old Testament reserves for God himself, Kyrios or Lord. In him is revealed the whole meaning of the word God, and indeed the whole meaning of the word man.

For his uniqueness does not consist in being inimitable. The whole tenor of the passage is that no one who refuses to do as he did has the right to call himself his follower. Let this mind be in you, Christians of Philippi or Finchley, which was in Christ Jesus, because you too are called to become what he became.

Paul and the Jews

In only one short section of this letter (for the christological text just quoted is really only a parenthesis) does Paul deal of set purpose with a theological matter. The warm and personal thank-you note to friends takes a sharp turn in chapter 3, where we find ourselves without warning in a controversy between Christianity and Judaism, with Paul suddenly[1] alerting his readers to the dangers of returning to Jewish practices. The subject is one which will occupy our attention in much of the next chapter, since the letters to Galatia and Rome, written shortly after this one, are almost totally concerned with this problem.

What is remarkable about Paul's words here is the strength of his emotional outburst. His bitter attack on Jewish religious practices displays a hostility which, however it is explained, is a distinct embarrassment fo the modern reader. He brands Jews in general as troublemakers and 'swine' – the rough modern equivalent of the Jewish term of abuse 'dogs' (Philippians 3:2). Their laws on what foods may or may not be eaten are summarily dismissed as 'belly-worship', and their sacred ritual of circumcision as 'phallus-obsession' (3:19). There is even a caustic play on words which warns Christians against the 'circum-scissors' (3:2).

Several comments are in order here. And the first is the obvious one that when members of a family have words, their language is likely to be far more outspoken, even savage, than they would tolerate from outsiders. Paul belonged to the Jewish family he is here attacking: he even boasts on this page of his 100% Jewish background (3:4–6). Non-Jews can only stand by in such a slanging match. They are not entitled to join in on the grounds that, because Paul abused the Jews, they may (some would even say must) do so too. They are not family. Christians should remember this when they are tempted to identify too easily with the prophets, in the Old Testament and New, who berate their own people.

Secondly, Paul's concern on this page is that of all the prophets of Israel, from Amos down to Jesus: the constant temptation of religious people to assess their relationship with

---

[1]   So suddenly, and with such a marked change of tone, that many scholars take chapter 3 to be part of a quite distinct piece of correspondence with Philippi, attached by Paul's editors to the otherwise simple bread-and-butter letter.

God by the extent to which they are 'practising'. Religion does not consist of its practices, rites or sacraments, less still is it to be identified with them. To be more concerned for observance than for the love, justice and forgiveness of which it should be a symbol, is to turn religion into an empty shell. Formalism in religion has always rightly called down the wrath of the prophet and the atheist alike, who see more clearly the one thing that ultimately matters, the need to heal people's brokenness so that they should become more fully human.

This having been said, it must be added that in this chapter Paul has clearly over-reacted. It is one thing to say that ritual is not everything, quite another to say that it is nothing, and may be ridiculed. The values by which a community lives are almost inevitably frittered away if they are not embodied in some external ritual. To attack Jewish practices as mercilessly as Paul does (and Matthew and John do not lag far behind him) may be explained as part of the zeal of a convert: it is not unknown for erstwhile lovers to become the bitterest of enemies. All the same, the New Testament authors should have been the first to speak with reverence of the ritual which enshrined the values that led them to Jesus of Nazareth. It was their intransigence which was to bring about a schism between Judaism and the emerging Christian community which was clearly quite beyond the intentions of Jesus himself. It is perhaps the price that the world must pay for having giants like Paul, that along with his great insights, it must also accept his great blind spots.

And yet that is not the whole story either. In the last analysis, the passionate language of this chapter is not to be explained simply in terms of a family quarrel, or of a horror of religious formalism or of a love-hate relationship between Christianity and Judaism. At the deepest level, Paul's overriding fear is that argument about detailed structures could obscure or even obliterate the very essence of the gospel.

There is a type of religion which places such emphasis on religious observances that God ultimately emerges as a demanding taskmaster whom it is difficult if not impossible to satisfy. At the heart of the story of Jesus is the good news that God is not like that. He does not demand satisfaction. People find union with him not by their own laborious efforts, but simply by becoming aware that he loves and accepts them even in their sins. No one can earn salvation; we can only accept it (this is what faith means) as a free gift.

This basic insight into the nature of God has constantly and successfully been pushed into the background by many Christians, whatever may be said about Jews. Paul is determined at all costs to keep it in the foreground, and to resist any attempt, whether from Jews or from Christians, to return to the self-justifying legalism which would smother it:

> I believe nothing can happen that will outweigh the supreme advantage of knowing Christ Jesus my Lord. For him I have accepted the loss of everything, and I look on everything as so much rubbish if only I can have Christ and be given a

> place in him. I am no longer trying for perfection by my own efforts, the perfection that comes from the Law, but I want only the perfection that comes through faith in Christ, and is from God and based on faith. (3:8–9)

It is Christ, and the insight he has learnt from him, that Paul is determined not to let slip from his grasp. It is the same Christ, still living on, that he is resolved to possess and be possessed by. It is the very reality of Christ that he is intent on reproducing in his own life:

> All I want is to know Christ and the power of his resurrection and to share his sufferings by reproducing the pattern of his death. That is the way I can hope to take my place in the resurrection of the dead. (3:10–11)

It is interesting to note how Paul's approach to Christianity has subtly changed over the five or six years since he wrote to the Christians of Salonika. There, the resurrection of the dead and the coming of Christ were realities that still lay in the longed-for future. Here, the future has become far less important than the present. Christ comes not at the end, but here and now, in the midst of life, as participation in his suffering necessarily flowers into a share in his resurrection. Christ is the very centre of Christian life, not only its goal.

This shift in focus from the future to the present, from the next world to this world, will become even more marked in Paul's later letters. He finishes his short theological treatise in this letter with a fine profession of faith in this world:

> (As Philippi is a colony of Rome, so) we are a colony of heaven, and from heaven comes the saviour we are waiting for, the Lord Jesus Christ, and he will transfigure these wretched bodies of ours into copies of his glorious body. (3:20–21)

Christians are not to think of themselves as holding passports for heaven; their passport is *from* heaven, commissioning them to live the life of heaven in this world. Christians are not to write off the world they live in as beyond redemption, or to imagine that souls must be rescued out of it. On the contrary the very fabric of the world, in all its bodiliness, must be rescued by being transformed. Christians are not to think of Christ as distant or far away from them in this task; he is present in their midst, filling them with confidence, peace and joy:

> Rejoice I say, rejoice I say,
> Again I say, Make holiday;
> Let people see your heart's at peace,
> The Lord's not far away.

Away with every anxious thought,
And bid your worries all depart;
In all your praying, let God see
A calm and grateful heart.

And then the very peace of God,
Whose depths will never be explored,
Will fill your heart and guard your mind
In Jesus Christ our Lord. (4:4–7, author's translation)

Paul and the Philippians

Yet the last word about the letter to Philippi must not be about its theology, which is more of a digression than its main theme. The letter is characterised not by its doctrinal teaching but by its personal tone, as I hope the quotations have shown. Nowhere else in his correspondence is Paul so open and self-revealing, and so tender, warm and affectionate, chained prisoner though he is. The Philippians had won a place in his heart which none of his other communities could claim, and he was able to expose himself before them with an unassuming simplicity which, in other contexts, might have invited only ridicule:

It is only natural that I should feel like this towards you all, since you have shared the privileges which have been mine... You have a permanent place in my heart, and God knows how much I miss you all. (Philippians 1:7–8)

Be united in following my rule of life. Take as your models everybody who is already doing this and study them as you used to study me. (3:17)

Keep doing all the things that you learnt from me... and have heard or seen that I do. (4:9)

For all the faults of this generous man, it is quite obvious that he won a place in the hearts of the Philippians as he has in the hearts of countless admirers since. That great aficionado of his, Catherine of Siena, puts it quite simply:

There never was anyone like the apostle Paul

or, as she affectionately calls him, *quel Paoluccio*, 'that darling Paul.'

FOR DISCUSSION

1. Paul sees the dying Jesus as an undistorting mirror of what God is really like – not a demanding taskmaster, but a servant who gives himself away. Is this, by and large, how God comes across to us in our dogmas, our moral teaching, our liturgy, our sermons, our personal prayers?

2. Are you happy with the suggestion that Paul had his blind spots, over which you are allowed to disagree with him? Would this be true of all the biblical authors? If so, how exactly does the Bible continue to be the Word of God to you?

3. Paul attacks his Christian and Jewish enemies boldly and mercilessly. In our ecumenical insistence on gentleness and tolerance, have we lost some deeper truth about love of neighbour?

6. To the Celts, and a Fair Copy (Galatians and Romans)

It has been the ambition of every Scripture scholar to write a commentary on Paul's epistle to the Romans. Some of the great ones have achieved this ambition: witness Origen, Chrysostom, Augustine, Aquinas, Luther, Calvin, Barth, Lagrange and Dodd.

The roll-call, needless to say, is not a naive attempt to reflect glory on the present chapter. On the contrary, it is an indication of the importance that has always been attached to this epistle. Together with the epistle to the Galatians, it has traditionally been regarded as the key to Paul's thought. Luther even added, 'and to Christianity,' so that he refused to accept as Scripture anything he thought inconsistent with these undisputed writings of Paul.

Which makes it obvious that what follows cannot begin to do justice to either of the epistles, let alone to the two of them in one chapter. But then I am not attempting to provide a commentary on them, only an introduction which may help readers find their way about them.

The Galatians

'Galatians' is an alternative form of the words Gallic and Celtic. The Galatians were a Celtic tribe originating in ancient Gaul or France, which was actually known as 'Galatia' by the Greeks. About three hundred years B.C. they migrated east across northern Italy, Yugoslavia and Bulgaria, and still calling themselves 'Celts' eventually settled around what is now the town of Ankara in northern Turkey. When they became part of the Roman Empire, they were grouped for administrative purposes with other tribes in southern Turkey to form what was know as the 'Province of Galatia'. In Paul's time, therefore, the word 'Galatians' could be used in two

EUROPE

OF GALATIA

●Ankara

GALATIA

ASIA

ROMAN PROVINCE

Antioch●

●Iconium

Lystra●

●Derbe

●Antioch

CRETE

Km

0 ⌐_____⌐ 300

Paul's First Journey 45AD

CYPRUS

different senses. In its strict sense it referred to the immigrant
Celts of the north; in its wider sense it included the people of
southern Turkey too.

If Paul used it in this second and wider sense, then the letter
to Galatia could be the earliest writing of the New Testament.
Paul had formed a Christian community among these southerners on his very first missionary journey in the year A.D.45. If
it was these he was here writing to, then the letter could be at
least ten years older than the correspondence we have been
considering in the last two chapters. What makes this unlikely
however is that it is closely related to the letter to Rome, which
was clearly written after the crisis at Corinth and the
correspondence that ensued. In fact, the letter to the church at
Rome is so clearly a fair copy of the one to the Christians of
Galatia (whether northerners or southerners) that it is difficult
to imagine they could have been separated by a gap of ten
years. They must have been written within months of each
other, because they both deal with the same problem and solve
it along the same lines. That is why I am treating both in the
same chapter. What distinguishes the two letters is that one
was written off the cuff, in the heat of the moment, the other
composed with great care in a calmer and more dispassionate
mood. The year was about A.D.57.

Christianity and Judaism

I pointed out in the previous chapter that the question exercising Paul at this stage of his missionary work was the precise relationship between the newly emerging Christian community and the Judaism out of which it was born. Could the daughter continue to live not only at peace with her mother, but in the ancestral house? Or was her outlook so basically different that she must go her own way and set up a separate home?

Should the followers of Jesus see themselves essentially as Jews (as Jesus certainly did), committed to the traditional Jewish way of life, whatever additional practices and beliefs they subsequently adopted? Should they become, as it were, a religious order within the general confines of Judaism? Or was their Christian experience so distinctive, and their claims for Jesus so absolute, that they could no longer be contained within Judaism? Were the Jewish and Christian visions of God so mutually exclusive that they must require each other's conversion, or extinction?

The first members of the Christian community were, like Jesus and his immediate disciples, all Jews. Not surprisingly, they saw the issue along the lines of the first of the alternatives suggested above, not the second. Christianity was no more than a branch of Judaism. It could not claim, as it did, to inherit the promises of the Old Testament unless it remained within the tradition of those by whom and for whom the Old Testament was written. And while recruitment continued to be restricted to fellow Jews, the community saw itself as an enclave within Judaism. There was no reason to think otherwise until, first in a trickle and then in a flood, pagan converts began to be attracted to the gospel. On what conditions were they to be admitted into this Christian community within Judaism?

Paul had no doubts, at least to begin with. For him, what Jesus of Nazareth had brought about was no mere reform movement within Judaism, but a radically new departure. If his followers did not exploit this newness and assert their independence of Judaism, they would betray the gospel's deepest insight and undermine its worldwide potential. His own policy, put into effect in his very first missionary journey among pagans, was to welcome them into the Christian community without any reference to the traditional Jewish practices which until then Christians had adopted as a matter of course. He claimed that the logic of the gospel demanded this.

Many of his fellow Christians were aghast. How dismiss the whole history of Judaism as if it stood for nothing? Jesus himself had found the will of God expressed in the Law of Moses, and had preached not its abrogation but its need to be brought to perfection. If Paul maintained that such a programme was untrue to the future, they asserted no less vehemently that his course of action betrayed the past. They were convinced that it would lead to disaster, and were vindicated by the subsequent history of those who were admitted to Christianity without undergoing a Jewish novitiate first. The tenuous grasp of the gospel, open immorality and even rank heresy of the church at Corinth could hardly have been possible in a community of converts from Judaism! Experiences like these only strengthened them in their resolve to protect the gospel from mavericks like Paul and maintain Christianity's close links with Judaism.

When Christians of this persuasion began to dog Paul's footsteps to rectify what they regarded as Paul's mutilated presentation of the Christian message, the issue came to a head. Paul's immediate reaction was one of outrage. But the situation forced him to analyse more closely the principles on which he had so far unquestioningly been working.

Being right with God

The zealous missionaries recently arrived in Galatia had persuaded Paul's new converts, apparently without great difficulty, that their Christianity was incomplete. Paul had omitted to circumcise them, and without circumcision they could not stand in a right relationship with God or take their place among the true people of God. But then Paul was a freelance latecomer. Unlike the Jerusalem apostles, the 'Acknowledged Leaders' (Galatians 2:6), he had not known the Jewish Jesus, and had only ever half grasped the meaning of the gospel.

This personal attack by fellow Christians stung Paul into his bitterest piece of writing. In typical over-reaction, he maintains that his interpretation of the gospel alone is totally right and theirs is totally false – in fact they are 'sham Christians and interlopers' (2:4). It is not only this Jewish-Christian libel which is evil and accursed, but the whole of Judaism (1:8, 3:13, 5:10). It is all Jewish practices that are a form of infantilism and enslavement (3:23, 4:9, 4:25, 5:1), not simply the magical reliance on them. In short, Paul's anger has made him polarise. He rightly establishes the dividing line which runs through the heart of every religion, indeed of every religious person, between obedience to God and disobedience, sincerity and hypocrisy, awareness and blindness, maturity and childishness – but decides that Christianity is totally on one side of the line, and Judaism totally on the other.

On circumcision in particular Paul is most vehement, since this was the practice on which he and his adversaries most disagreed. 'They only want to make a fair show in the flesh,' says Paul, with a tasteless play on words (6:12). Even more scurrilously, he advises his readers to 'tell those who are disturbing you I would like to see them castrate themselves', with the cruel suggestion that the venerated Jewish ritual is a piece of savagery like that practised by the eunuch priests of Cybele (5:12). It is almost as if Paul the present-day Christian is embarrassed by the past that has marked him out, indelibly, as a Jew.

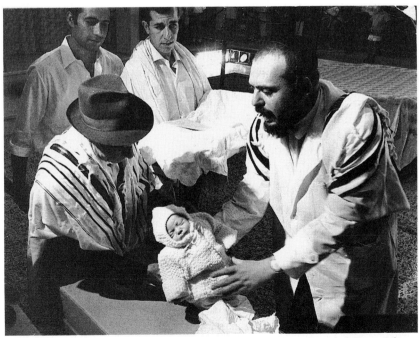

Barnaby's Picture Library

The comments made in the previous chapter, when the letter to Philippi already touched on this problem, are apposite here too. In the first place, we are again in the presence of a family quarrel. Neither Paul nor his adversaries would thank us for supporting them or cheering them on, for this is a dispute between Jews – even though they have both become Christians. If their words are extreme, that is a matter between brothers, and brothers (not to mention sisters) have been known to join forces to turn on any outsider who thought they could take sides.

But Paul's anger is over something more basic than a family quarrel. His concern here, as it was at Philippi, is to hold on to the gospel's central message. To the question, 'How does the human race achieve a right relationship with God?', many people would reply, 'By obeying God's commands.' People's right standing with God is a result of their own efforts. Certainly there was a strong tendency in the Judaism of New Testament times (indeed it is to be found in religious people of all times) to answer the question in those terms. The answer which Jesus gave was quite different, though many of the Jewish prophets who preceded him had said the same: 'People achieve a right relationship with God by accepting it as a free gift from God.'

In the first answer, people have to prove themselves in a life-long struggle. In this struggle they do not, of course, work without God's 'grace'. Still it is by their own efforts (aided though they be) that they make their way to God, and they may demand their final union with God as a right, as something they have earned. They become good because *they* are good.

In the second answer, people have no need to prove themselves. God accepts them as they are, with all their sins. They are forgiven and have free access to God even before they turn their back on their sins. When they acknowledge that this is so, of course, they will make every effort to live a life of union with God. Still it is God's unearned love, not their own effort, that puts them right with God. They become good because *God* is good.

The first answer lays stress on human responsibility and the seriousness of the task, but at a cost. The service of God becomes a system of rule-keeping, and fosters an attitude of self-sufficiency in those who imagine that God is thereby beholden to them.

The second answer is not without its dangers for those who understand it frivolously, but it maintains the supreme sovereignty of God. It sets people gloriously free from any system which would enslave them.

Jesus, as I have said, was not the first or the only voice to proclaim the good news of this second answer. The prophets of all times and places have never ceased to recall their people to this vision of a reality that is ultimately gracious, not least the prophets of Israel. In the heat of the argument, Paul overstates his case by making Christianity the sole visionary of this truth, and fabricating a Judaism which has always been totally blind to it. He may even be arguing against the overstrict views he himself once held, rather than against any official Jewish position.

Yet there is no denying that, at least in positive terms, he has seized the heart of the gospel, that God's forgiving love is not to be hedged about with conditions. It is given gratis to all who admit that they cannot earn it, and who open themselves to receive it as a free gift. This gospel is good news for all people, and is not to be restricted to a chosen élite.

There were many in Jesus' time who found such a vision of God literally too good to be true, since its demands ('Go thou and do likewise') were too awful to envisage. It should be no surprise that Paul aroused opposition when he preached the same gospel. It still arouses considerable resistance today, not least among professed Christians, when they are told that right relationship with God is not established by the keeping of a law, however sacred, or by their own efforts or 'works', but by the freely given love of a gracious God. Yet only those who accept that vision of God as the ruling principle of their lives can be said to live by faith.

The Church of Rome

In terms of 'standing in the right relationship with God' therefore, or 'justification' as it is here called in lawyer's language, the letter to Galatia has forced Paul to analyse more closely the meaning of the Christian message. God has been revealed in the life, teaching and death of Jesus as the forgiveness of the world's sins. This must be proclaimed to all people without distinction, or they might continue to imagine themselves unforgiven. The mere acceptance of this good news will transform their lives.

This interpretation of Christianity, forced out of Paul under torture, as it were, and marred therefore by inevitable exaggerations, formed the rough draft of the more balanced letter which he sent shortly after to the church of Rome. He was in Corinth at the time, and nearing the end of his third great missionary journey. His plan, after returning to Jerusalem, was to embark on a fourth journey which would take the gospel further west than he had so far been able to venture. Amazing man that he was, he mentions that he has his mind set on Spain (Romans 15:23). Beyond that, in the world he knew, there were only fish to preach to. For such a project in the western Mediterranean, Rome was the natural base to operate from. The Galatian letter, pruned of its polemic, amplified and more calmly rewritten, would sum up for the Christians of Rome what he believed in and where he stood, and prepare them for his arrival.

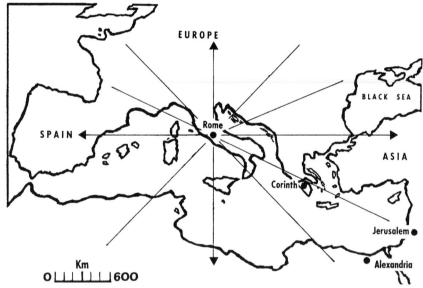

Why Paul should have thought it necessary, or useful, to send such a full statement of his faith to a church not of his founding, is not immediately clear. In the other great headquarters which he had so far operated from – Salonika, Corinth and Ephesus – he had himself founded the Christian community, and taken personal responsibility for the problems which arose there later. But the church of Rome was founded by others, and he is very aware that he must not give the impression of trying to build on their foundations (Romans 15:20). Indeed, that is the very thing he has complained of others doing to him!

What then was the purpose of the letter? Was it simply to win the approval and support of a church which so far had never met him in person but only knew of him by repute? Or was it to allay their suspicions of someone beginning to get a name as a dangerous innovator? Or was it to present a carefully documented defence of a missionary policy which had over the years aroused so much opposition?

Or was the reason more closely linked to the Galatian crisis which had so recently racked Paul? Like other churches, the Christian community in Rome had at first been composed entirely of converts from Judaism, but their predominance was gradually eroded by the influx of converts from paganism. Did Paul feel that the ensuing tension was at least partly his responsibility, as the officially designated 'apostle of the Gentiles'? Certainly it is his concern in the letter to Rome to stress, more explicitly than in the Galatian correspondence, the continuity between the New Testament and the Old, so that Jewish Christians might see his gospel not as a repudiation of Judaism but as its fulfilment, and their Gentile brethren come to a deeper appreciation of the Jewish stock on to which they have been grafted.

For whatever precise reason Paul wrote to the Romans, his letter remains the nearest attempt he ever made to analyse his faith systematically, and for that reason it will always have pride of place among his epistles. In later letters he will explore his Christian vision from other angles, but never so fully or so meticulously as he does here.

Paul's self-defence (Galatians 1–2)

The extent to which the letter to the Galatians is a less systematic piece of theology may be gauged from its opening words. The address is no sooner on the envelope, as it were, than Paul charges into his topic, hands flailing. Even the customary paragraph of prayer and praise, *de rigueur* in all his other letters, is omitted: the matter is too urgent. Certain people in Galatia had questioned his presentation of the Christian message, and it is essential that he put the record straight. He must show that it is their preaching, not his, which is a travesty of the gospel:

From Paul, an apostle who does not owe his authority to *any human being*... but who has been appointed by Jesus Christ himself... To the churches of Galatia... I am astonished at the promptness with which you have turned away from the one who called you and have decided to follow a *different* version of the Good News... Some troublemakers among you want to *change* the Good News of Christ... Some who do *not* really belong to the brotherhood have furtively crept in to spy on the liberty we enjoy in Christ Jesus, and want to reduce us all to slavery... Let me warn you that if anyone preaches a version of the Good News *different* from the one I have already preached to you, whether it be me or even an angel from heaven, he is to be cursed!... The Good News I preached is not a *human* message that I was given by any *human* being, it is something I learnt only through a revelation of Jesus Christ. (Galatians 1:1–12, 2:4)

And for two chapters Paul presents a detailed autobiography to show how his dispute with Peter – no doubt being quoted by the opposition to discredit Paul – was in face a vindication of Paul's interpretation of the gospel. Yes, he admits, there was disagreement between the two, but on a matter of practice not of teaching. Yes, he admits, he did challenge Peter ('I opposed him to his face' 2:11), but this was not an attack on his authority. On the contrary, it was a most striking acknowledgement of it: of all people, Cephas the Rock must remain firmly grounded in the gospel's insights, and not mislead his brethren by actions inconsistent with them.

It has often been suggested that the Christianity which eventually spread through the western world was an invention of Paul's, and that his complex religion distorted and stifled the simple Christianity originally preached by Jesus and his disciples. These chapters give the lie to such a charge; this is precisely the accusation Paul is here answering. He volunteers to go into the dock, and invites all comers to challenge the fact that, when it came to the point, the Jerusalem apostles could only agree that he had rightly interpreted the gospel. There is no denying that Paul's zeal in planting Christian communities in every major city of the Mediterranean ensured that the Christianity which took root in the world of his time would have a distinctively 'Pauline' flavour. But if he had thought that this was something radically different from what was preached by Peter, James and John, he could never have written these chapters.

How God puts right what is wrong (Galatians 3–5, Romans 1–3)

The point at issue between Paul and his critics is 'justification'. How are people 'justified', or put right with God? If the purpose of our life is to be righteously related to a righteous God, how is such righteousness achieved? Both letters here under discussion devote their main attention to this question.

The letter to Galatia expresses Paul's thought on the subject in strongly emotional terms. What witchcraft could make people turn away from the gospel's totally satisfying answer to this question and grope for unnecessary answers (indeed, illusory ones) in a childish system of rule-keeping?

Anna Dimascio

Are you people of Galatia mad? Has someone put a spell on you to make you take your eyes off the crucifixion of Jesus Christ, displayed before you like an advertisement hoarding... Was it because you practised the Law that you received the Spirit, or because you believed the gospel preached to you? Are you foolish enough to end in outward observances what you began in the Spirit? Have all the favours you received been wasted?

Once you were ignorant of God, and enslaved to 'gods' who are not really gods at all; but now that you have come to acknowledge God – or rather, now that God has acknowledged you – how can you want to go back to elemental things like these, that can do nothing and give nothing, and be their slaves? You and your special days and months and seasons and years! You make me feel that I have wasted my time with you...

You once welcomed me as an angel of God, as if I were Jesus Christ himself. What has become of this enthusiasm you had? I swear that you would even have gone so far as to pluck out your eyes and give them to me. Is it telling the truth that has made me your enemy?...

My children! I must go through the pain of giving birth to you all over again, until Christ is formed in you. I wish I were with you now so that I could know exactly what to say; as it is, I have no idea what to do for the best...

I, Paul, tell you this: if you allow yourselves to be circumcised, Christ will be of no benefit to you at all... If you look to the Law to make you justified, then you have separated yourselves from Christ...

You began your race well: who made you less anxious to obey the truth? You were not prompted by him who called you!... Tell those who are disturbing you (with talk of the need for circumsion) I would like to see the knife slip! (Galatians 3:1–4, 4:8–20, 5:2–12)

For Paul, the revelation at the heart of the gospel is of a God who loves and freely forgives. The life, preaching and especially the death of the man Jesus had shown Paul as never before, that God did not condemn him for the sinner that he was, but accepted him. To remain bound to a system of law-keeping after that would equivalently be to refuse to accept that God *is* like that, and to reject the death of Jesus as the ultimate affirmation that God is as forgiving as that figure on the cross. Henceforward right relationship with God could no longer depend (if it ever did depend) on satisfying the demands of a harsh taskmaster. It could only be achieved by accepting, in faith, the free forgiveness of the loving God revealed in the death and resurrection of Jesus Christ.

This insight, shouted out with such urgency in the letter to Galatia, is expressed in more measured terms in the letter to Rome. Indeed, its opening sentence is so meticulous in its wording, and so completely rounded in its formulation (unlike modern versions it contains no full-stops), that it has figured for centuries as one of the principal readings for Advent:

From Paul, a servant of Christ Jesus who has been called to be an apostle, and specially chosen to preach the Good News that God promised long ago through his prophets in the Scriptures. This news is about the Son of God who, according to his human nature, was a descendant of David: it is about Jesus Christ our Lord who, in the order of the spirit,

the spirit of holiness that was in him, was proclaimed Son of God in all his power through his resurrection from the dead. Through him I received grace and my apostolic mission to preach the obedience of faith to all pagan nations in honour of his name. You are one of those nations, and by his call belong to Jesus Christ. To you all, then, who are God's beloved in Rome, called to be saints, may God our Father and the Lord Jesus Christ send grace and peace.
(Romans 1:1–7)

The new understanding of God so often hinted at in the Old Testament and finally made concrete in the New; the death and resurrection of the man Jesus in which that understanding was most clearly expressed; the compulsion to proclaim this liberating message to a Roman world stunted by its cramped images of God – all that is contained in this fine opening sentence, to form a perfect summary of the letter that follows.

And the same measured tone marks the two subsequent chapters, where Paul calmly analyses the situation of a world, both pagan and Jewish, which does not know Christ. That the pagan world of the time is helplessly imprisoned in its sinfulness is, for Paul, hardly worth arguing. He simply writes out a list that speaks for itself. Anyone who has read the Roman history of the time, or seen television presentations of it, will vouch that the list, though selective, is not untrue to life. But for all their privileges, the Jews have not been able to escape this sin of the world. All that their Mosaic Law has been able to do for them, according to Paul, is to point out to them more clearly than to others, the helplessness of the situation.

Where to turn? There is nowhere to turn except to God. Human helplessness is God's opportunity. When people's best efforts have led to an impasse, God reveals his Christ. When people realise that they cannot earn their own righteousness, however hard they try, they find the God who gives them their righteousness as a free gift.

The only response people can make to such a revelation is to acknowledge their own powerlessness and to commit themselves to the power of God. This response Paul calls 'faith'. Faith is the recognition of the pitiful inadequacy of our own effort, achievement, merit or 'works', and the joyful acceptance of a right relationship with God as sheer grace, freely bestowed on all comers. People who have spent a lifetime keeping the law (or even The Law) have only this advantage over outlaws:

they know more poignantly than all others how desperately they need the revelation of the God who shines on the face of Christ, to lift the burden from which no system of law-keeping can set them free.

The Gospel preached to Abraham (Galatians 3, Romans 4)

At this point in both letters, Paul introduces the story of Abraham. It reads at first sight like an enormous irrelevance, especially in its fine detail about Sarah and Hagar, and the 430 years intervening between Abraham and the Law of Moses. In fact, given the circumstances in which these letters were written, the choice of the story is a masterstroke. For a readership newly aware of the importance of Moses, Paul points even further back in Jewish history to Abraham as an illustration of the very point he wishes to make. For the story of Abraham is a kind of anticipation of the story of the gospel.

The cycle of Abraham stories is introduced into the book of Genesis to highlight the free initiative of God. The 'fall' of Adam and Eve (Genesis 1–3), echoed in the 'falls' of Cain (chapter 4), of the sons of God (chapter 6),of the contemporaries of Noah (chapters 6–9) and of the citizens of Babel (chapter 11) – all this forms a deliberately dark background against which chapter 12 will stand out: the intervention of the Saviour God to rescue mankind from chaos and to make a new beginning.

Like a new Adam one man is chosen, and he receives the divine promise already made to Adam, that mankind is destined for God's blessing, not his curse. This promise will stand, against all human indications to the contrary, because it is made by a God who brings life out of death, whether it be the dead womb of Sarah, or Isaac's dead end on the mountain. All that is asked from Abraham is faith – the total commitment of himself to a God who can and will do just that.

The story of Abraham is the story of that commitment. He is the counterpart of Adam who refused to commit himself. His obedience to the call to leave the security of his homeland, his blind venture into an unknown country, his willingness to lead the unpromising life of a nomad, his acceptance of his impotent old age, his readiness to sacrifice his only son on demand – all these were illustrations of his faith. And that faith was his 'justification' or right relationship with God. He had done the very opposite of earning his salvation by his own efforts. He had simply opened himself to the God who alone

John Fisher

can save. God 'justifies' sinners, not those who imagine they have earned their right relationship with him.

The conclusion which Paul draws from the Abraham saga is this. If anyone wants to appeal to Abraham as the Father of God's People, let him go the whole hog. Like father, like son. It is absurd to claim to be a true son of Abraham if you are not like him in the one particular which characterized him: the faith which established him in the right relationship with God. And clearly this has nothing to do with race. Those who live their lives by faith in such a God are pure Abrahamites; those who do not are fakes, whatever their physical genealogy.

That is why the words in the opening paragraph of the Abraham story were a sort of prophecy: 'In you all nations (and not only your physical descendants) will be blessed.' They form a kind of vignette of the gospel ('The gospel was proclaimed to Abraham'), because the preaching of Paul is based upon exactly the same good news – the free gift of salvation to all men, pagans as well as Jews, who commit themselves to the image of God revealed in the Abraham stories.

What then shall we say about Abraham, the ancestor from whom we are all descended? If Abraham was justified as a reward for doing something, he would really have had something to boast about, though not in God's sight because scripture says: 'Abraham put his faith in God, and this faith was considered as justifying him.' If a man has work to show, his wages are not considered as a favour but as his due; but when a man has nothing to show except faith in the one who justifies sinners, then his faith is considered as justifying him...

And this was before he had been circumcised, not after; and when he was circumcised later it was only as a sign and guarantee that the faith he had before circumcision justified him. In this way Abraham became the ancestor of all uncircumcised believers, so that they too might be considered righteous...

The promise of inheriting the world was not made to Abraham and his descendants on account of any law but on account of the righteousness which consists in faith... What fulfils the promise depends on faith, so that it may be a free gift and be available to all of Abraham's descendants, not only those who belong to the Law but also those who belong to the faith of Abraham who is the father of all of us.

Scripture says: 'I have made you the ancestor of many nations.' Abraham is our father in the eyes of God, in whom he put his faith, and who brings the dead to life and calls into being what does not exist. Though it seemed Abraham's hope could not be fulfilled, he hoped and he believed, and through doing so he did become 'the father of many nations'... Even the thought that his body was past fatherhood – he was about a hundred years old – and Sarah too old to become a mother, did not shake his belief. Since God had promised it, Abraham refused either to deny it or even to doubt it, but drew strength from faith and gave glory to God, convinced that God had power to do what he had promised. This is the faith that was 'considered as justifying him'.

Scripture however does not refer only to him but to us as well when it says that his faith was thus 'considered'; our faith too will be 'considered' if we believe in him who raised Jesus our Lord from the dead. (Romans 4:1–24)

Abraham 'put his faith in God, and this faith was considered as justifying him'. Don't you see that it is those who rely on faith who are the sons of Abraham? Scripture foresaw that God was going to use faith to justify the pagans, and proclaimed the Good News long ago when Abraham was told: 'In you all the pagans will be blessed.' Those therefore who rely on faith receive the same blessing as Abraham, the man of faith.

On the other hand, those who rely on the keeping of the Law are under a curse... Christ redeemed us from the curse of the Law by being cursed for our sake... so that in Christ Jesus the blessing of Abraham might include the pagans, and so that through faith we might receive the promised Spirit. (Galatians 3:6–14)

Christian freedom (Galatians 4–5, Romans 5–8)

The image of God glimpsed in the Abraham stories and openly revealed in the gospel is a totally liberating one. The word which describes God best is not 'accountant' but 'love'. He does not hold people's sins against them but freely forgives them. He will receive the guilty with as genuine a welcome as the innocent and treat them as if they had never wandered from him. The realisation that this is so brings a sense of relief, peace, and above all freedom, which no system of lawkeeping can ever bring. The crushing burden of self-justification is lifted. The tedious and never-ending task of trying to make ourselves just in the sight of God is over. The liberating good news is that right standing with God cannot be earned, by whatever human or superhuman effort. Indeed, it doesn't need to be earned, because it is freely bestowed on all who will accept it. Paul expresses the wonder of it as he concludes the 'dogmatic' part of these two letters:

> Through our Lord Jesus Christ, then, by faith, we are judged righteous and at peace with God... By faith and through Jesus, we have entered this state of friendship with God, in which we can boast about looking forward to God's glory... Our hope is not deceptive, because the love of God has been poured into our hearts by the Holy Spirit which has been given us... We are filled with joyful trust in God, through our Lord Jesus Christ, through whom we have already gained our reconciliation. (Romans 5:1–11)

> Before faith came, we were allowed no freedom by the Law; we were being looked after till faith was revealed. The Law was to be our guardian until the Christ came and we could be justified by faith. Now that that time has come we are no longer under that guardian, and you are, all of you, sons of God through faith in Christ Jesus... The proof that you are

sons is that God has sent the Spirit of his Son into our hearts: the Spirit that cries, 'Abba, Father', and it is this that makes you a son, you are not a slave any more... When Christ freed us, he meant us to remain free. Stand firm, therefore, and do not submit again to the yoke of slavery... In Christ Jesus whether you are circumcised or not makes no matter – what does matter is having faith... My brothers, you were called, as you know, to liberty. (Galatians 3:23 – 5:13)

Those who are in Christ Jesus are not condemned, because the law of the spirit of life in Christ Jesus has set us free from the law of sin and death... The Spirit of God has made his home in you... If Christ is in you then your spirit is life itself because you have been justified... He who raised Jesus from the dead will give life to your own mortal bodies through his Spirit living in you... The spirit you received is not the spirit of slaves bringing fear into your lives again; it is the spirit of sons, and it makes us cry out, 'Abba, Father!'... With God on our side, who can be against us?... When God acquits, could anyone condemn?... Nothing can come between us and the love of Christ, even if we are troubled or worried, or being persecuted, or lacking food or clothes, or being threatened or even attacked... For I am certain of this: neither death nor life, no angel, no prince, nothing that exists, nothing still to come, not any power, or height or depth, nor any created thing, can ever come between us and the love of God made visible in Christ Jesus our Lord. (Romans 8:1–39)

The sense of freedom and confidence in these passages is overpowering. It contrasts strongly with the fearful and cramped image of themselves which most Christians convey to outsiders. As long as there are Christians who find it difficult to say with Paul, 'I am *free* of law', they will need to read and re-read these apparently obsolete pages, for they will not yet have seized one of the gospel's most basic insights.

This is not to say that law can be dispensed with. Codes and rules will always be neccessary to classify the many ways in which the needs of others may make demands on us, or to bring order into things which might otherwise dissolve into chaos, or even simply to reduce to routine the less important aspects of life. But no one must imagine, says Paul, that any such code can capture the will of God. The message of the gospel is that right relationship with God cannot be acquired by the keeping of a law, however venerable, because law can never do more than determine a person externally. To that extent, law stunts and enslaves, and from that cramping slavery the gospel offers liberation.

It is misleading, therefore, to speak of the gospel (as even Paul is guilty of doing) as the 'New Law'. It does indeed claim to supersede the 'old' system of law, but not simply by being another and better law! It would be ironic if people applauded the courage of Jesus in breaking through the legalism of his day with his bold 'You have been taught... but *I* say', and then sheepishly accepted his sayings as law in order to call themselves his followers. One can only follow Jesus by doing what he did, which is to be free and mature enough to make one's own decisions.

True Christians see themselves as freed from any merely external determination. They are animated by another principle of action altogether, known variously as the Spirit of God, the Spirit of Christ or the Holy Spirit. This is nothing other than a Christlikeness which consists of knowing God as Jesus knew him. True Christians are self-determined, and therefore free, because they have put on another self which recognises the absolute demands of the only absolute, love.

Colourfully, Paul speaks of the Spirit with which the Christian is endowed as the 'first-fruits' (Romans 8:23) – the first sheaf which guarantees that the rest of the harvest is to follow. Elsewhere he uses the even more striking metaphor of the 'first instalment' or 'down payment' which puts God under

Eastern Daily Press

obligation, as it were, to honour his promise. It is significant in this respect that, in these pages, Paul should so frequently speak of salvation in the present tense. For Christians, union with God is not something in the dim and distant future to which they are making their uncertain way. On the contrary, they already have one foot in heaven, because they already have the Spirit of Christ dwelling in their heart. And in the light of that experienced love of God, anything that the future may hold, even death itself, fades into insignificance.

The Jewish question again (Romans 9–11)

It was the need to re-think the relationship between Judaism and Christianity that sparked off the two letters of Paul here under discussion. In the argument we have so far followed, the thorny question has never been far beneath the surface. But before concluding the letters with some pieces of practical advice, Paul makes one more attempt, and a lengthy one, to come to grips with the problem (Romans 9–11).

It is unlikely that these chapters were originally composed for inclusion in the letter: they can be omitted without disturbing the sequence of thought which links chapter 8 to chapter 12. They read more like a set piece, perhaps a sermon, which Paul has used on other occasions. He includes it here because it analyses the question more calmly and dispassionately than the circumstances of the letter to the Galatians allowed. To that extent it makes amends for some of that letter's more emotional outbursts.

Not that these chapters could be called cold or abstract. The problem they try to solve is one which racks Paul. One could read his letter to Galatia and hardly be aware that Paul was himself a Jew. Not so these chapters:

> What I want to say now is no pretence; I say it in union with
> Christ – it is the truth – my conscience in union with the
> Holy Spirit assures me of it too. What I want to say is this;
> my sorrow is so great, my mental anguish so endless, I would
> willingly be condemned and be cut off from Christ if it could
> help my brothers of Israel, my own flesh and blood. They
> were adopted as God's sons, they were given the divine glory
> and the covenants; the Law and the ritual were drawn up for
> them, and the promises were made to them; they are
> descended from the patriarchs, and from their flesh and
> blood came Christ who is above all. (Romans 9:1–5)

This ardent opening paragraph states the problem succinctly. If all that has been said in the preceding chapters about 'being right with God' is correct, then was the whole of the Old Testament a waste of time? If in the last analysis there is no difference in the eyes of God between Jews and pagans, then what was God's purpose in choosing a People? If Israel's long and glorious history ended in rejecting the gospel which was meant to be its climax, then what was the point of it all? Paul's willingness to barter his own salvation for an answer to this question is some indication of how intractable he regards it to be.

He has no glib solution to offer, therefore. Over the course of three chapters he wrestles, thinks aloud, struggles with inadequate words, and explores the areas which might throw a little light on the darkness which surrounds him: God's unquestionable freedom and sovereignty, the inevitable scandal of his selectivity, his patient tolerance of evil, his overriding mercy. Paul's confusion may be gauged from the fact that he refers easily to Israel's failure, disobedience, unfaithfulness, blindness and defection, yet remains adamant throughout that 'God has *not* rejected his people' (11:1), that 'the Jews have *not* fallen for ever' (11:11), that 'the chosen people are *still* loved by God' (11:28), that 'God *never* takes back his gifts or revokes his choice' (11:29), that in short God remains a God of *mercy*, not of revenge (11:32).

Not surprisingly, therefore, Paul's, final answer to the problem he has set himself is that there is no answer. And indeed, in the terms in which he has posed it (either conversion to Christianity or damnation), the problem is insoluble. In fact, when people were told, as Francis Xavier's first audience in China were reputedly told, 'All your ancestors are in hell', they are entitled to reply, 'Then that is where we want to be too.'

So within his limited terms of reference, Paul cannot understand why Israel fails to recognise the revelation of God he himself has recognised in Jesus. But he is confident that God understands, for he is a God who cannot refuse to Israel the love he has shown to the whole pagan world. To that inscrutable mystery of God, Paul like Job can only bow his head:

God has imprisoned all men
in their own disobedience
only to show mercy to all mankind.

How rich are the depths of God
- how deep his wisdom and knowledge –
and how impossible to penetrate his motives
or understand his methods!
Who could ever know the mind of the Lord?
Who could ever be his counsellor?
Who could ever give him anything
or lend him anything?
All that exists comes from him;
all is by him and for him.
To him be glory for ever! Amen. (11:32–36)

Advice on Christian living (Galatians 5–6, Romans 12–15)

Paul concludes his two letters, as always, with some pages of practical advice. The pages that have gone before, abstract and speculative as they may occasionally seem, are not to be dissociated from the practical everyday question of Christian behaviour; one flows naturally from the other. Theology is not for theologising but for living.

It is because the gospel has revealed God as mercy, forgiveness, acceptance and love that the believer must 'go and do likewise'. Not to do so would equivalently be unbelief – the refusal to acknowledge mercy, forgiveness, acceptance and love as the 'ultimate'.

To put it in other words, Paul's insistence that those who take the gospel seriously must see themselves as being free of law may not be construed as a general invitation to self-indulgence, irresponsibility or indifference. The opposite is true. To acknowledge love as the absolute in one's life, and to be under its inner compulsion instead of under the merely external constraint of law, is to acknowledge a call to a far deeper maturity than any rule-keeping will ever be able to foster. And of course, in passing, the very behaviour which the law tried to ostracize by force will be excluded as being inconsistent with love anyway:

If you love your fellow men you have carried out your
obligations. All the commandments: You shall not commit
adultery, you shall not kill, you shall not steal, you shall not
covet, and so on, are summed up in this single command:
You must love your neighbour as yourself; that is why it is
the answer to every one of the commandments.
(Romans 13:8–10)

> The whole of the Law is summarised in a single command:
> Love your neighbour as yourself. (Galatians 5:14)

The letter to Galatia deals with this topic in terms of the fundamental distinction between 'flesh' and 'spirit'. These two words do not mean what our words 'body' and 'soul' usually mean[1]. It is the whole person, not simply our body, that is 'flesh' insofar as we are weak and vulnerable, alienated from the God who is the source of all life and power. Similarly it is the whole person, body and soul, who is (or can be) 'spirit' insofar as we are attuned to God and open to the guidance of his 'Holy Spirit', that is to say, the spirit of love revealed in the life and death of Jesus of Nazareth. To be truly free, not only in theory but in practice, to be really liberated from the slavery of self-justification, people must resist the never-ending demands of their 'fleshly' self, and follow the dictates of their 'spiritual' self. Under that guidance, they will have no more need of a law to put them right with God. For with a love like Christ's own (the analysis Paul makes is remarkably similar to his famous 'portrait of Christ' in 1 Corinthians 13), the egoistic self is like him dead on the cross, where law can make no more claims:

> If you are guided by the Spirit you will be in no danger of yielding to self-indulgence (the flesh), since self-indulgence is the opposite of the Spirit... If you are led by the Spirit, no law can touch you. When self-indulgence is at work the results are obvious: fornication, gross indecency and sexual irresponsibility; idolatry and sorcery; feuds and wrangling, jealousy, bad temper and quarrels; disagreements, factions, envy; drunkenness, orgies and similar things... What the Spirit brings is very different: love, joy, peace, patience, kindness, goodness, trustfulness, gentleness, and self-control. There can be no law against things like that, of course (nor *for* them, either!). You cannot belong to Christ Jesus unless you crucify all self-indulgent passions and desires. Since the Spirit is our life, let us be directed by the Spirit.
> (Galatians 5:16–25)

---

[1] It is because they have normally been taken as equivalents of body and soul, with disastrous results, that modern versions generally offer a paraphrase. The Jerusalem Bible finds the word 'flesh' so elusive that in translating the letters to Galatia and Rome it has used a dozen different paraphrases, sometimes three in the same verse (cf. Romans 8:3). The New Jerusalem Bible (1985) manages to reduce these to two.

Feuds and wrangling   Barnaby's Picture Library

The treatment in the letter to Rome is longer, but it is based on
the same fundamental principle, namely the new 'mind' or
'self' to which those who accept the gospel's understanding of
God have logically committed themselves:

> Think of God's mercy, my brothers, and worship him... Do
> not model yourselves on the behaviour of the world around
> you, but let your behaviour change, modelled by your new
> mind. (Romans 12:1–2)

People cannot honestly call themselves Christians unless they
have the 'mind' of Christ, and like Christ show unconditional
love to their fellow men and women:

> Do not let your love be a pretence, but sincerely prefer good
> to evil. Love each other as much as brothers should, and have
> a profound respect for each other... If any of the saints are in
> need you must share with them; and you should make
> hospitality your special care. (12:9–13)

This love must be extended even to enemies:

> Bless those who persecute you: never curse them, bless them... Treat everyone with equal kindness... Never repay evil with evil but let everyone see that you are interested only in the highest ideals. Do all you can to live at peace with everyone. Never try to get revenge... If your enemy is hungry, you should give him food, and if he is thirsty, let him drink. (12:14–20)

Christians must show love above all to members of the community with views that differ from their own:

> If a person's faith is not strong enough, welcome him all the same without starting an argument... Far from passing judgement on each other, therefore, you should make up your mind never to be the cause of your brother tripping or falling. (14:1,13)

Under this last heading Paul devotes as much as a chapter and a half to a single problem, because it brings him back to the Jewish Question which has informed the whole of his writing. The problem itself – how to treat converts from Judaism who continue to observe their kosher laws – has no great relevance for the modern reader. But the principle on which Paul solves it has – the need to treat others as we know God in Christ has treated us:

> Meat-eaters must not despise the scrupulous. On the other hand, the scrupulous must not condemn those who feel free to eat anything they choose, since God has welcomed them... The one who eats meat does so in honour of the Lord; but then the man who abstains does that too in honour of the Lord... But if your attitude to food is upsetting your brother, then you are hardly being guided by charity. You are certainly not free to eat what you like if that means the downfall of someone for whom Christ died...
>
> The kingdom of God does not mean eating or drinking this or that, it means righteousness and peace and joy brought by the Holy Spirit... Do not wreck God's work over a question of food. Of course all food is clean, but it becomes evil if by eating it you make somebody else fall away. In such cases the best course is to abstain from meat and wine and anything else that would make your brother trip or fall or weaken in any way...

Each of us should think of his neighbours and help them to become stronger Christians. Christ did not think of himself... May he who helps us when we refuse to give up, help you all to be tolerant with each other, following the example of Christ Jesus... Treat each other in the same friendly way as Christ treated you. (14:3–15:7)

The attitude of reverence and respect for Judaism, the insistence that the Roman converts from paganism are grafted on to a Jewish root, not vice versa – this contrasts strongly with Paul's earlier summary dismissal of Jewish practices as 'belly-worship' (Philippians 3:19) and 'a waste of time' (Galatians 4:11). But then, as has become clear throughout our analysis, the letter to Rome represents not the usual extempore Paul, but Paul at his most balanced and well considered. Witness its closing paragraph which, like the one with which the letter began, is a masterpiece of compression and integration:

Glory to him who is able to give you the strength to live according to the Good News I preach, and in which I proclaim Jesus Christ, the revelation of a mystery kept secret for endless ages, but now so clear that it must be broadcast to pagans everywhere to bring them to the obedience of faith. This is only what scripture has predicted, and it is all part of the way God wants things to be. He alone is wisdom; give glory therefore to him through Jesus Christ for ever and ever. Amen. (16:25–27)

The sequel

From what I have said in appreciation of the letters to Galatia and Rome, it does not follow that they were as warmly appreciated by those to whom they were written. As regards the crisis in Galatia, we have no record to tell us whether it was successfully solved, or what sort of Christianity, Pauline or anti-Pauline, flourished there after the letter was received. About Rome too we are largely ignorant. The letter's last chapter lists the names of twenty-eight people to be personally greeted, many among them women, and commentators have spoken enthusiastically of Paul's 'positive genius for friendship'.[2] But in a church which Paul has not yet visited, some of these (perhaps many) may be simply names he knows of by hearsay. Manuscript evidence even gives support to the theory that the list is of Paul's friends in Ephesus, not Rome, and that it may be no more than a covering note for a copy of the Roman letter forwarded to that city. The facts are that when Paul did arrive in Rome he was a desperately lonely man (2 Timothy 4:9–13), and that when he was finally imprisoned and on trial for his life he wrote (or was plausibly represented as writing): 'There was not a single witness to support me. Every one of them deserted me' (4:16).

It remains true nonetheless that the letters to Galatia and

UNRWA photo by M.Nasr

Rome are Paul's most mature writings, the ripe fruit of twenty years of thought and work, of preaching, suffering and experience. They were written when he was at the height of his

---

2   The warm and personal tone of these greetings is well brought out by the following translation, which has worked hard to find names close to the originals but with a twentieth-century ring about them: 'Say hello to Prissy and Adrian, my co-workers for Christ Jesus. They stuck their necks out to save my life, and for this not only am I thankful but all the churches as well. Greetings also to the church that meets in their home. Hello to my dear Ellwood... And hello to Mary, who worked so hard for you. Warm regards to Andy and Junior, my kinfolks and fellow captives, who are highly respected in ministerial circles. Best wishes to Ansley, so dear to me in the Lord. Greetings to Howard, our Christian co-worker, and my dear Stocky. Regards to Everett, a true Christian. Say hello to the Harris Baker family. Hello, Cousin Helena. Hello to the faithful Nicholson family. Greetings to Truman and Trudy, the Lord's workers. Say hello to dear Pearl, a hard worker for the Lord if ever there was one. Remember me to Rufus, a prince of a Christian, and to his mother – and mine. Give my love to Austin, Herb, Perry, Herman and the brothers with them. Much love to Frank and Julia, and to Nero and his sister, and to Ollie and all the other Christians with them. Give everybody a big hug. All of Christ's churches greet you. (Clarence Jordan, *The Cotton Patch Version of Paul's Epistles*, Association Press, New York, 1968, p. 45)

powers and, unknown to himself, had completed his active missionary work. No other writings in the New Testament, the gospels excepted, have influenced subsequent Christian thought as deeply.

FOR DISCUSSION

1. If you think that (at least generally speaking) you stand in a right relationship with God, do you think of it primarily as your own work or God's?

2. Has your Christianity given you, as Paul hoped, a sense of freedom to make your own mature decisions? If it hasn't, whom would you blame?

3. As a Christian, how do you regard Jews? As convert material, or as brothers and sisters who have different views from your own? With respect? With fear? With pity?

7. Letters from Jail
(Colossians and Ephesians)

Paul ended his letter to the Christians in Rome with a request for prayers that he 'may escape the unbelievers in Judaea' (Romans 15:3). He was obviously expecting trouble. The subsequent account of his further journeys in the Acts of the Apostles shows how right he was. He had no sooner reached Jerusalem from Corinth (where he had penned that prayer) than the Jewish conspiracy which had dogged his footsteps throughout his missions caught up with him. On the pretext that he was desecrating the Jerusalem temple, he was almost lynched, and although he was temporarily rescued by the Roman guard, the Jewish charge of disturbing the peace stuck, and he was imprisoned. After three useless years in jail in Jerusalem and Caesarea, he lodged an appeal for trial before the emperor, to which as a Roman citizen he was entitled. So he finally achieved his ambition of reaching Rome, but it was in chains. The two letters to Christians in Colossae and Ephesus – the 'Captivity Epistles' as they are known – were written from his Roman jail, about the year A.D. 61–62.

Asian angels
Colossae and Ephesus are towns in Asia Minor, the modern Turkey. Paul had set up Christian communities there on his third missionary journey nearly ten years earlier. In fact he had chosen Ephesus, the capital of the Roman province, as his headquarters for three years and, as we have seen, had written the letters to Corinth and Philippi from there.

According to the Acts of the Apostles he had said farewell to the young Asian churches with words of deep foreboding:

> I know quite well that when I have gone fierce wolves will invade you and will have no mercy on the flock. Even from your own ranks there will be men coming forward with a

travesty of the truth on their lips to induce the disciples to follow them. (Acts 20:29–30)

No doubt in this case the words were written with hindsight, but they represent accurately enough the agonising dilemma which faced Paul at every turn: the possibility that what he regarded as the pure gospel would later be distorted by missionaries who saw Christianity in terms different from his own. His fears had been confirmed in Salonika, Corinth, Philippi and Galatia. In each case the world has been permanently enriched by Paul's anguished attempts to see the gospel afresh, now from this angle, now from that, and to restructure it in order to counteract the dangers that he saw threatening it.

The threat that invaded Asia after his departure, and to which the letters here under discussion are a response, was gnosticism. We have already encountered this phenomenon in chapter 4, where we saw how a gnostic interpretation of Christianity stung Paul into writing his anguished letters to Corinth. But in Corinth gnosticism was on foreign soil. Its real home, as numerous New Testament writings with Asian connections bear witness (John's gospel and epistles, Timothy, Jude, 2 Peter, Revelation) was Asia Minor, where the ancient religious thought of the East was beginning to make an impact on the West.

Gnosticism is so called because it speaks of union with God in terms of 'gnosis' or knowledge. People's wretchedness and sense of alienation is due to ignorance. What they need is the knowledge which will reveal to them their real situation, and release them from the illusory world in which they are imprisoned. Gnosticism offered them this secret knowledge. Sometimes it took the form of an all-embracing philosophy which, in its comprehensiveness, claimed to solve the riddle of the universe. More often it took the form of the ritual re-enactment of a myth, in the course of which the mystery hidden from the rest of the human race was disclosed to the initiated. Asia Minor was renowned for the variety of its 'mystery religions'.

We have already seen, in the case of Corinth, how easy it was to present Christianity (or a passable version of it) in these gnostic terms. It was even possible, in the setting of Asia Minor, to interpret Judaism in these terms, and to present the Jewish understanding of God and man as a 'mystery' superior to all others. In this case the transcendent God of traditional Judaism became a being so remote that union with him was impossible except through the mediation of angels.

Most of the Old Testament had been content with one such intermediary, known as 'The Angel of the Lord'. Gnostic Judaism so isolated God from the material world of daily experience that they required many more, and gladly imported them from the East under the grandiose titles of 'Thrones, Dominations, Principalities, Powers and Authorities'. These provided a hierarchical order whereby Infinity could be gradually diluted to the finite world's taste and whereby, conversely, the godless world could slowly emerge from its earthbound state and by degrees ascend to God.

When Jews with persuasions of this kind became Christians, it was almost inevitable that they should see Jesus as one of these go-between angels, the highest no doubt, but still only an intermediary between earth and heaven, himself belonging naturally to neither. And the ancestral Jewish Law, far from being a light to guide the human race, was seen in almost entirely negative terms, as a programme for suppressing the unreedemable body in which the human race was imprisoned. It is this curious combination of the Corinthian gnostic understanding of Christianity, and of the Galatian Jewish interpretation of it, that forms the background to Paul's letter to the Christians at Colossae. The operative words in the following passage have been italicised:

> Make sure that no one traps you and deprives you of your freedom by some secondhand, empty, rational *philosophy* based on the principles of this world instead of on Christ. In his body lives the *fulness of divinity*... He is the head of *every* 'Sovereignty' and 'Power'.
>
> In him you have *been* circumcised... He has *overridden the Law*... *He has done away* with it by nailing it to the cross; and so he *got rid* of the 'Sovereignties' and the 'Powers'...
>
> From now onwards, never let anyone else decide what you should eat or drink, or whether you are to observe annual festivals, New Moons or sabbaths. These were only pale reflections of what was coming: *the reality is Christ*. Do not be taken in by people who like grovelling to *angels* and worshipping them... If you have really died with Christ to the principles of this world, why do you still let *rules* dictate to you?... 'It is *forbidden* to pick up this, it is *forbidden* to taste

that, it is *forbidden* to touch something else'; all these prohibitions are only... an example of *human* doctrines and regulations... with their self-imposed devotions, their *self-abasement*, and their severe treatment of the *body*. (Colossians 2:8–23)

The letter to 'the Ephesians'

The passage just quoted is pure Paul. In its jerky sentences, its biting edge, and its hard-hitting polemical tone it is closely akin to the other letters of Paul we have so far considered. And it contrasts strongly with the serene, highly dignified and almost lyrical tone of the Ephesian letter, with which the Colossian letter is usually associated. The contrast is well illustrated in the poem with which the letter begins. The original contains only one full-stop, and is perhaps too circular and complex for many westerners to appreciate. The following rendering may convey something of its rhythmical quality;

Blessed be the God whom Jesus called Father,
To him be glory and praise.

In Christ we are already in heaven;
In Christ, before the world began,
God chose us as his holy people,
As the loving brothers of Christ.
   This was the gracious purpose of God;
   To him be glory and praise.

In the Christ of his love he has loved us,
In Christ's death he has freed us from sin;
So richly his grace he has lavished,
So freely his secret shared.
   This was the gracious purpose of God;
   To him be glory and praise.

In Christ God's plan is laid open,
In Christ time has come to an end;
For all things, on earth and in heaven,
Are to be made whole in Christ.
   This was the gracious purpose of God;
   To him be glory and praise.

In Christ, the God who guides all things,
Who rules all events and all time,
Chose one out of all of the nations

As the first to hope for Christ.
   This was the gracious purpose of God;
   To him be glory and praise.

In Christ this good news of salvation
Has spread to the nations of the world;
They too have received Christ's Spirit
As the pledge that heaven is theirs.
   This was the gracious purpose of God;
   To him be glory and praise.
      (Ephesians 1:3–14, author's translation)

The letter of which this magnificent poem forms the opening lines is related to the letter to Colossae in something of the same way that Romans is related to Galatians. In both cases the letters presume the same background, and passages in one are often repeated word for word in the other. But the later letter not only omits the controversial tone of the earlier, it is also far more relaxed and leisurely in style. The later one seems to be a fair copy of the earlier, presenting the same matter in a calmer and more balanced way.

UNRWA photo by M.Nasr

In the case of the letter to 'the Ephesians', the tone is so calm that it is almost impersonal, as if the letter had been written by someone who did not know the addressees in person. The greetings, good wishes and advice it contains are so general-ised that they will fit any Christian readership of the time. In fact the most important manuscripts leave a blank at the italicised words in the address on the envelope, 'To the saints who are *at Ephesus*', as if the letter was really a circular into which each local community could insert its own name.

Is this so 'un-Pauline' that the Ephesian letter must be regarded as a brilliant forgery? Or is it the later work of a disciple of Paul, anxious to make his master's teaching available for wider consumption? Or is it, in spite of all the difficulties mentioned, a genuine letter of the imprisoned Paul, a mellower and more contemplative Paul admittedly but, now that the fighting is over, able to restructure the positive content of his letter to Colossae, and make a final confident synthesis of what the Christian gospel means to him?

Scholars differ in their response to this question. Many are content, quite simply, to leave it open.

Christ for gnostics

In trying to combat a gnostic interpretation of Christianity, Paul is labouring under several difficulties. In the first place, the all-embracing world-view of gnosticism has revealed to him how narrow his own brand of Christianity could sound. True enough he had been one of the first to grasp the gospel's universal potential, and it was largely due to his vision that its message had been carried to every corner of the world of his time. All the same, in the light of the magnificient sweep of gnostic philosophy, the kind of controversy in which he had recently been engaged – whether Christianity was for Jews only or for everyone, and under what conditions – must have sounded positively provincial.

On the other hand, when enthusiastic Asian Christians had tried to widen the scope of the gospel in gnostic terms, they had simply mutilated it. They had wanted to put Jesus on the religious map by according him a place among a hierarchy of celestial intermediaries. But this not only removed him from the brotherhood of men and women – and so made him useless as their saviour – but it also fell pitifully short of what needed to be said about him. For however gorgeous the titles of these heavenly hierarchies, and however grandiose the rank of these semi-gods, he was something infinitely more:

> He sits at God's right hand in heaven, *far* above every 'Sovereignty', 'Authority', 'Power' or 'Domination', or any *other* name that can be named, not only in *this* age but also in the age to *come!* (Ephesians 1:21)

> Everything visible and everything invisible – 'Thrones', 'Dominations', 'Sovereignties', 'Powers' – *all* things were created through him and for him. (Colossians 1:16)

> The 'Sovereignties' and 'Powers' must learn, through the *Church*, how comprehensive God's wisdom really is! (Ephesians 3:10)

> He got *rid* of the 'Sovereignties' and the 'Powers', and paraded them in public, *behind* him in his triumphal procession! (Colossians 2:15)

> We have to struggle *against* the 'Sovereignties' and the 'Powers' who originate the darkness in this world! (Ephesians 6:12)

Christ is no mere angel or semi-god. He is the very image of the invisible God, a window through which men can finally see without distortion God as he really is. The heart of the Christian gospel is that God is no longer to be thought of as distant, inaccessible, remote from the world. In the man Jesus, the gap has been for ever closed.

Yet in saying that gnostic Christians have not done Christ justice, Paul knows that he himself is in danger of overstatement, and wrestles with the problem which Christian theology must always face – how to speak of the 'divinity' of Christ without selling his humanity short. Paul preserves the fine balance by claiming that Christ reveals not only who God is, but also what man is, and can be. He is not an afterthought in creation, but its very template. He is man as God planned him to be, the model on which not only the human race but the whole of creation is based, the principle upholding the whole of the cosmos. So he comes into our midst as the beginning of a new creation, the New Man around whom all things will find their cohesion and fulfilment. In Christ, the physical and material world, far from being opaque to God, has been revealed as the open gateway to the world of God:

> In Christ Jesus, you that used to be so far apart... have been brought close. (Ephesians 2:13)

> Through him, both of us (Jews and pagans) have in the one Spirit access to the Father. (Ephesians 2:18)

> We are bold enough to approach God in complete confidence, through our faith in Christ Jesus. (Ephesians 3:12)

But the principal difficulty which Paul has to face is one with which every controversialist is familiar – the fact that he has to play his match away, not at home. The terms in which the contest is waged are not necessarily those which he would have spontaneously chosen; they are laid down by the opposition. And in his anxiety to show that Christianity has nothing to fear in being compared with gnosticism, Paul himself has to present the gospel, willy nilly, as a kind of superior gnosticism.

We have already noted this feature in the Corinthian correspondence, where gnostic terminology, instead of being repudiated, is (reluctantly?) accepted and used. In the Colossian and Ephesian letter there is no further reluctance; a single sentence can contain as many as seven technical terms from gnosticism:

> May your *understanding* come to *full* development, until you really *know* God's *secret* in which all the jewels of *wisdom* and *knowledge* are *hidden*. (Colossians 2:2)

Anyone examining the ten short chapters of this correspondence will find them punctuated with the same words, or with synonyms like 'mystery', 'revelation', 'depths', 'fulness', 'perception', 'insight', 'enlightenment', 'hidden self'. The challenge has been boldly taken up. If those are the rules of the game, Paul will play along, and explain Christianity in terms of eternal mysteries revealed and heavenly secrets disclosed:

> It was by a revelation that I was given the knowledge of the mystery... If you read my words, you will have some idea of the depths that I see in the mystery of Christ. This mystery that has now been revealed through the Spirit to his holy apostles and prophets was unknown to any men in past generations... I, who am less than the least of all the saints, have been entrusted with this special grace, not only of proclaiming... the infinite treasure of Christ but also of explaining how the mystery is to be dispensed. Through all

the ages, this has been kept hidden in God... so that the 'Sovereignties' and 'Powers' should learn... how comprehensive God's wisdom really is, exactly according to the plan which he had from all eternity in Christ Jesus our Lord. (Ephesians 3:3–11)

Since Paul has so boldly borrowed gnostic terminology, it seems only fair to point out that his words may not be 'absolutised'. That is to say, the language used in these letters is not the only language in which the gospel may be presented. Indeed Paul had the right to expect other generations to make the effort he had made to speak to their contemporaries in their language, not someone else's. So, for instance, it was appropriate when presenting the mystery of Christ to gnostics to speak of the *Pleroma* or 'Fulness' as dwelling in him, since this was then a technical term referring to the total reality possessed by God, a reality existing only in more and more diluted form in the intermediaries emanating from him. But for an age which has long since abandoned the imagery of divine emanations, the word 'fulness' can only be misleading, except as a reminder that fidelity to the gospel demands that the uniqueness of Christ must be discovered in and through his manhood, not in something added to it.

So much needs to be said to justify the following translation of the poem with which Paul sums up his presentation of Christ for gnostics. Like other poems in Paul's letters, it may be only a quotation of an already existing hymn.

In him we knew a fulness
never known before;
In him we saw a man fully
living.

In him we see the God who
can't be seen;
In him all things that will be
or have been
Have roots and take their
being.
  In him we knew a fulness
  never known before;
  In him we saw a man fully
  living.

John Fisher

The universe, and all its millions teeming,
Seen and unseen, in him find their meaning,
Their reason and their value.
  In him we knew a fulness never known before;
  In him we saw a man fully living.

He lives in those who, breathing with his breath
- Source of their life, and conqu'ror of their death –
Together form his body.
  In him we knew a fulness never known before;
  In him we saw a man fully living.

Through him alone a world by sin defiled
Finds its forgiveness, and is reconciled,
His death our peace and healing,
  In him we knew a fulness never known before;
  In him we saw a man fully living.
      (Colossians 1:15–20, author's translation)

In short, when speaking to first century gnostics Paul had to say that Jesus possessed the fulness of divinity. Twentieth century agnostics need far more to be assured that Jesus posssessed the fulness of humanity. One statement is not trying to say anything different from the other.

The Church as Christ's body
In that hymn, Paul has touched on another aspect of what he spoke of as 'the depths I see in the mystery of Christ'. For the church, the community of Christ's followers, is part of that mystery. Indeed it is the very body of the cosmic Christ he has so far been describing.

Paul has already, in the letters to Corinth and Rome, spoken of the church as the body of Christ, in order to emphasise the unity and harmony required of Christ's disciples. That note is sounded in these letters too, and frequently. But the metaphor is further extended to make Christ the head of this body, and this is understandable in a context where so much stress is put on the role of Christ as the source of life, growth and direction.

Yet 'metaphor' is the wrong word. For Paul does not call the church the 'body of Christians' but the 'body of Christ'. He does not envisage the church as an entity separate from the risen Christ. It is the very resurrection body of that Christ, the means by which the Jesus whose physical body died on the cross remains embodied in the world. Indeed Paul so identifies the church with Christ that he sees the very divinity he attributes to Christ necessarily overflowing into the church:

> (God) put everything in subjection beneath his feet, and appointed him as supreme head to the church, which is his body and as such holds within it the fullness of him who himself receives the entire fullness of God.
> (Ephesians 1:22–23, N.E.B.)

For Paul, the church cannot be described in terms other than those he has already used to speak of Christ himself – the New Man, the human race as God originally designed it, the beginning of a new creation:

> He is the peace between us (Jews and Gentiles), and has made the two into one and broken down the barrier... to create one single New Man in himself out of the two of them... to unite them both in a single body.
> (Ephesians 2:14–16)

All the aspects here mentioned (unity, head of the body, divine fulness, the new creation) are brought together in the following fine passage:

> The saints together make a unity in the work of service, building up the body of Christ. In this way we are all to come to unity in our faith and in our knowledge of the Son of God, until we become the perfect Man, fully mature with the fulness of Christ himself... If we live by the truth and in love, we shall grow in all ways into Christ, who is the head by whom the whole body is fitted and joined together... So the body grows until it has built itself up, in love.
> (Ephesians 4:12–16)

In short, the divine secret which Paul feels constrained to make public to the whole Mediterranean world is not summed up in the word 'Christ' but in the word 'church'. For the church is not, as some would have it, a coterie, or a fellowship, or a movement, or an organisation, or a corporation, or a firm ('Holy Mother Limited' as one cynic called it). It is God's master-plan for making people truly human. Paul sees it as the breathtaking revelation of how all human beings, chosen or not, privileged and underprivileged, can become one:

> If you read my words, you will have some idea of the depths I see in the mystery of Christ. This mystery that has now been

revealed... means that Gentiles now share the same inheritance, that they are parts of the same body, and that the same promise has been made to them, in Christ Jesus, through the gospel... I have been entrusted with this special grace, of proclaiming to the Gentiles the infinite treasure of Christ... Through all the ages this has been kept hidden in God... so that all should learn only now, *through the church,* how comprehensive God's wisdom really is. (Ephesians (Ephesians 3:4–10)

The parallel passage in the letter to Colossae is more succinct, and even more expressive:

God made me responsible for delivering God's message to you, the message which was a mystery hidden for generations and centuries and has now been revealed to his saints... in order to show all the rich glory of this mystery to Gentiles. The mystery is *Christ among you,* your hope of glory. (Colossians 1:25–27)

Throughout these passages, Paul perseveres with the gnostic language to which he has committed himself – mystery, hidden, revelation, wisdom, knowledge, fulness. But the extent to which he finally repudiates any thoroughgoing gnostic interpretation of Christianity may be assessed from the emphasis he puts on the totally human reality of Christ and the church. The Christ he speaks of in such glowing terms is not some disembodied figure out of the skies, but a carpenter from Nazareth. The glorious risen body of that Christ is not some ethereal ghost, but the everyday community of Ephesian businessmen and Colossian farmers. It is here on earth that redemption, salvation, glory and union with God are achieved, not in some imaginery otherworld or afterworld.

Heaven now

Several of the texts quoted have introduced what is called a 'realised eschatology': the *eschata* or 'last things' (death, resurrection, heaven, salvation, redemption, union with God, glory) are spoken of as realities to be encountered here and now, and not simply when life has come to an end. This way of speaking features elsewhere in Paul's letters, especially in Romans, but never so strongly as in these two. In contrast with Paul's earlier writings, where so much emphasis was placed on the future coming of Christ as the fulfilment of God's plans, the emphasis is now on the present. Christ's 'coming' is not even mentioned any more; all the hopes that concept once contained are now realised in the human race's union with Christ in the church. There the new world has already begun. The good news has been turned into the present tense. The list is impressive:

The Father *has made* it possible for you to join the saints and with them to inherit the light. (Colossians 1:12)

God *has taken* us out of the powers of darkness, and *placed* us in the kingdom of the Son that he loves, and in him we *possess* our redemption. (1:12)

All things *are reconciled* through and for Christ... he *has made* peace by his death on the cross. (1:20)

The mystery *has now* been revealed. (1:26)

In Christ's body lives the fulness of divinity, and in him you too, here and now, *find* your own fulfilment. (2:9)

You *have been* buried with Christ when you were baptised; and by baptism too you *have been* raised up with him through your belief in the God who raised him from the dead. (2:12)

Barnaby's Picture Library

You were dead in your sins... God *has brought* you to life with Christ, by forgiving you your sins. (2:13)

The Father of our Lord Jesus Christ *has blessed* us with all the spiritual blessings of heaven in Christ. (Ephesians 1:3)

Through the blood of Christ *we possess* our redemption. (1:6)

He *has* let us know the mystery of his purpose... to bring everything together under Christ, as head. (1:9–10)

You *have been* stamped with the seal of the Holy Spirit. (1:13)

The church *holds* within it the fullness of him who himself receives the entire fullness of God. (1:23, N.E.B.)

When we were dead (like Christ), God *brought* us to life with Christ. (2:5)

God *raised* us up with Christ, and *gave* us a place with him in heaven. (2:6)

By grace you *have been* saved, through faith. (2:8)

Through Christ, we *have* access to the Father. (2:18)

The mystery *has now* been revealed. (3:5)

Through the church the wisdom of God is *now* made known. (3:10)

We are bold enough to *approach* God in complete confidence. (3:12)

In this context it is interesting that the church, which in 2 Corinthians 11:2 and Revelation 21:2 is spoken of as only betrothed to Christ in the present, the marriage feast being reserved for the future, becomes in this letter a bride already wedded to Christ. The ideal marriage between God and the human race is not simply a consummation devoutly to be wished; it is already in some ways realised:

Husbands should love their wives just as Christ loved the church and sacrificed himself for her... so that when he took her to himself she would be glorious... A man must leave his father and mother and be joined to his wife, and the two will become one body. This mystery... applies to Christ and the church. (Ephesians 5:25–32)

It could be objected that there is something rather unrealistic about such language, that all these present tenses are in fact subjunctives or futures because they really speak of the church as it should or perhaps will be, not as it miserably is. Paul is well aware of the objection. He does not play down the fact that the church has to prove that it really *is* the body of Christ, by being Christ-like, by holding fast to its head, by growing, by loving, not least by suffering. There are plenty of future tenses and imperative moods in these letters. But the future must not be allowed to supplant the present, and everyday life must not be regretfully dismissed as a vale of tears. Heaven is now, because Christ is now. Paul's advice to his readers is never based on a hope of what they might become, but always on the reality of what they already are. The balance is nicely struck in the Easter epistle:

> Since you have been brought back to true life with Christ, you must look for the things that are in heaven, where Christ is, sitting at God's right hand. Let your thoughts be on heavenly things, not on the things that are on the earth, because you have died, and now the life you have is hidden with Christ in God. But when Christ is revealed – and he is your life – you too will be revealed in all your glory with him. (Colossians 3:1–4)

The life of Christians is here and now located in heaven, which is where the Christ to whom they are united is. Their resurrection is not something that they still hopefully wait for, it has already happened. What they do still wait for is the clear revelation that this is so. But this can only make plain what, in the darkness of faith, they should know is already a reality.

Homely advice

The two letters end, as all Paul's letters do, with a section of advice based on the preceding chapters. Paul's theology is never mere abstract theorising; it is heavy with practical implications. As I have just pointed out, his letters always follow the pattern: 'This is what you are; now *be* it.

It is because Christians constitute the very body of the Christ he has been extolling that they must be acutely sensitive to the least thing that could affect the health of that body:

> Bear with one another charitably, in complete selflessness, gentleness and patience. Do all you can to preserve the unity

of the Spirit by the peace that binds you together. There is
one body, one Spirit, just as you were all called into one and
the same hope when you were called. (Ephesians 4:2–4)

So, he continues, rivalry is self-evidently exluded, as well as
quarrelling, immorality, thieving, spitefulness and careless-
ness – for all these can only harm the body. In fact, he
concludes:

From now on, there must be no more lies: You must speak
the truth to one another, since we are all parts of one
another. (Ephesians 4:25)

If Christians are truthful to their neighbours, it is not because
they are so commanded, but simply because the opposite
would be sheer idiocy. Their neighbours are part of the same
body, and to deceive them would simply be to deceive oneself.

Perhaps the most famous page in this section of the letters is
the one which deals with Christian marriage. Its originality is
not always appreciated. The use of the word 'marriage' to
illustrate the relationship between God and men is not new; it
occurs frequently in the teaching of the prophets and of Jesus.
What is new is the way in which Paul turns this usage back to
front. We had thought that human marriage was a way in
which we could speak, metaphorically, of God's union with the
human race. Paul says that it is really the other way round. It is
human marriage which is the metaphor. The true reality , the
exemplar of which every human marriage is only an imperfect
copy, is the union between God and the human race. And that
original model, that unique love of God which would draw all
people into his embrace, of which every other union of two in
one flesh from Adam and Eve downwards has only been an
echo, is finally revealed in all its fulness when we see the body
of Christ, where God and the human race have become one
flesh, a body which lives on as the church. In the church the
marriage between God and creation is consummated. And of
that prototype Christian marriage should be a replica, a mirror
in which we may see the indescribable love of God for the
human race. When husband and wife grow in their love for
each other, that is not something which conflicts with their
spiritual life. That *is* their spiritual life:

The wife should surrender to her husband as if to Christ,
since he is her head, just as Christ is the head and saviour of

Barnaby's Picture Library

his body, the church. Just as the church surrenders to Christ, so should the wife surrender in all things to her husband.

The husband on his side, as a counterpart to that surrender, to evoke the surrender, should (not dominate his wife, or lord it over her, but) love his wife in the way that Christ loved the church. It was for the church that he gave himself up in order to bring it to God... It is in this way that the husband should love his wife, as if she were his own body... which he takes such care to nourish and keep free from harm. For this is precisely how Christ loves us, the

limbs that make up his body, the church. The book of Genesis spoke of a man leaving his father and mother in order to be united to his wife in one flesh. These words contain God's eternal secret, the secret that has finally been revealed in the union between Christ and his church.
(Ephesians 5:22–32, authors paraphrase)

It is interesting that Paul remains true, to the very end, to the gnostic language he has adopted . In the correspondence with Corinth he had felt the need to depreciate 'gnosis' in order to proclaim the superiority of love. Here he is quite content to end as he began proclaiming the value of 'gnosis', and even yearning for it to be deepened, because the God whom he has presented in the pages that have gone before can only be truly 'known' by loving. In the last analysis, faith and love are not alternative ways of union with God. For the Christian, at least, they are the same.

This, then, is what I pray... that Christ may live in your hearts through faith, and then, planted in love and built on love, you will with all the saints have strength to grasp and know, in all its breadth and length and height and depth, the love of Christ (though it is beyond all knowledge), and so be filled with the utter fulness of God. (Ephesians 3:14–19)

If we live by the truth and in love, we shall grow in all ways into Christ... So the body grows until it has built itself up, in love. (Ephesians 4:15–16)

In short, people cannot claim to know the mystery revealed in Christ unless they commit themselves to make that knowledge the pattern on which they model their own life:

You must live your whole life according to the Christ you have received. (Colossians 2:6)

You have stripped off your old behaviour with your old self, and you have put on a new self which will progress towards true 'gnosis' the more it is renewed in the image of its creator; and in that image there is no room for distinction between Gentile and Jew, or between... slave and freedman. There is only Christ... Bear with one another; forgive each other as soon as a quarrel begins. The Lord has forgiven you; now you must do the same. (Colossians 3:9–13)

Be friends with one another, and kind, forgiving each other as readily as God forgave you in Christ. Try, then, to imitate God... and follow Christ by loving as he loved.
(Ephesians 4:32–5:1)

So Paul presents his final synthesis of the gospel, as it has matured in his mind in the year A.D. 61–62, convinced that this will satisfy all the searchings of the Mediterranean world for a comprehensive philosophy of life. All human longings are answered in Christ, in whose life and death is revealed the eternal purpose of God. He gives meaning to the rest of humankind, and indeed to the whole of creation, as its model and point of reference. He continues to be embodied in the world in the community of those who believe in him – the church. Filled with his fulness, this community has its head, as it were, in heaven, yet stands squarely in the world as a sign of God's loving presence among people, and as the beginning of a new world, the model of what all men and women can and should be.

Perhaps the reason why the letters of Paul are so little read by Christians is that the contrast between his sublime vision and the pitiful reality is too painful.

FOR DISCUSSION

1. These epistles have placed considerable emphasis on a 'realised eschatology', in which all the eschata or last things (resurrection, heaven, glory) are no longer simply in the future, but experienced here and now. In what aspects of your life have you experienced 'resurrection', 'heaven' and 'glory'?

2. Paul's language in these epistles is so idealistic that it could be dismissed as unreal – 'Who could ever live up to this?' Is he making impossible demands? Should he have been more realistic?

3. Paul speaks of the community of Christians as an embodiment of Christ. Which aspects of our life as a Church make this claim most credible, and which aspects least credible?

8. To the Clergy
(Timothy and Titus)

The three short letters to be considered in this final chapter are
known collectively as the Pastoral Epistles because, unlike the
letters of Paul which we have been looking at over the last five
chapters, they were written not to communities at large, but to
individuals about their pastoral duties to the community. The
first letter to Timothy offers advice to a close companion of
Paul, who had been left in charge of the Christian mission
based on Ephesus. Not surprisingly, it presumes the same
background as the letters to Asia Minor analysed above, of a
Christianity threatened by a curious amalgam of philosophical
gnosticism and puritanical Judaism. The letter to Titus is
almost a copy of this one, for the benefit of another disciple of
Paul placed in a similar situation in Crete. The second letter to
Timothy presumes a slightly later date, with Paul expecting
death on the block at any moment.

Forgeries?
But are they Paul's letters at all? Every scholar, even the most
conservative, expresses more reservations about the au-
thorship of the Pastoral Epistles than about any other letter
with Paul's name on it.[1]

The reasons for this are many. Among them is the fact that
the letters refer to an itinerary of Paul very similar to the one
related in the closing pages of the Acts of the Apostles, but
diverging from it in all sorts of minor details. If the journey
was a genuine one, it could only have taken place after Paul's
Roman imprisonment. Yet the impression given by the closing
pages of Acts is that Paul only came out of prison in the year

---

[1] No such reservations are any longer expressed about the Epistle to the
Hebrews, which all scholars agree is not the work of Paul. It does not even
carry his name. That is why no reference has been made to it in this book.

A.D. 62 in order to go to his execution for the charges brought against him.

Are these letters then forgeries? Many scholars think so, though they would jib at the twentieth-century overtones of that word. More sympathetic to the culture of Paul's time, they draw attention to the accepted custom whereby a disciple felt entitled to spread his master's message by publishing the sort of letter he thought the master might have written had he still been alive. In that case the Pastoral Epistles would be 'pseudonymous writings', like the Second Letter of Peter and (some think) the Letter to the Ephesians.

Others are more reluctant, and suggest that it is not impossible that Paul was released from prison in Rome in the year 62. In that case he could have made the journeys referred to in these letters, before being captured a second time, and executed in the year 67. So the letters could be genuinely his – even if a secretary was given a freer hand than usual in the drafting of them – and would represent Paul's last words to the disciples who have to continue his work in Ephesus and Crete after his death.

Readers might like to make their own mind up on this question, since a good case can be made for both sides. Whatever conclusion they come to, they are assured of being in good company.

Backseat driving

One conclusion no one can avoid is that, after the Captivity Epistles considered in the foregoing chapter, these three letters can only come as an anticlimax. In the light of the breathtaking vision of Christianity enshrined in the letters from jail, this correspondence with the clergy is a bit of a disappointment.

To begin with, the author of the letters, whoever he might be, does a good deal of backseat driving. This is not entirely untypical of Paul, as we have seen in other letters of his. But the worried concern about the disciple's ability to cope here verges on the neurotic. The quotations speak for themselves:

> Timothy, my son, these are the instructions I am giving you: I ask you to remember the words once spoken over you... My advice is that, first of all, there should be prayers offered for everyone... I want the men to lift their hands up reverently in prayer, with no anger or argument. (1 Timothy 1:18 – 2:8)

I direct that women are to wear suitable clothes and to be dressed quietly and modestly, without braided hair and jewellery or expensive clothes. (2:9)

A presiding elder... must be temperate... not hot tempered... He should not be a new convert... It is also necessary that he be held in good repute by outsiders. (3:1–7) (Good criteria, though Paul himself might fail such a test!)

Deacons must be respectable men whose word can be trusted, moderate in the amount of wine they drink. (3:8)

Do not let people disregard you because you are young, but be an example to all the believers... Make use of the time until I arrive by reading to the people, preaching and teaching... Take great care about what you do and what you teach. (4:12–16)

Do not speak harshly to a man older than yourself... Treat the younger men as brothers and older women as you would your mother. Always treat young women with propriety, as if they were sisters. (5:1–2)

Enrolment as a widow is permissible only for a woman at least sixty years old who has had only one husband... Do not accept young widows... They learn to be gossips and meddlers in other people's affairs. (5:9–13)

Barnaby's Picture Library

The older women should... show the younger women how they should love their husbands and love their children, how they are to be sensible and chaste, and how to work in their homes, and be gentle, and do as their husbands tell them. (Titus 2:3–5)

Tell the slaves that they are to be obedient to their masters and always do what they want without any argument. (2:9)

You should give up drinking only water and have a little wine for the sake of your digestion and the frequent bouts of illness that you have. (5:23)

One can appreciate the fatherly solicitude behind such words of wisdom, but they seem to leave very little to the initiative of the disciple.

In line with that anxiety to solve all his disciple's problems is the theology of the three letters. Elsewhere, Paul's theology was always being hammered out in controversy and illustrated with living examples taken out of his own ministry. Here, in contrast, a kind of *rigor mortis* has set in. Again and again the admonition is solemnly given to teach only orthodox 'sound doctrine', to cling to trusted formulas, and to 'guard the deposit'. This is no doubt a good thing, but it effectively dissipates the fiery exuberance and sense of bold originality which characterises all Paul's letters. It also made it possible for later generations to imagine that all the answers to their questions were contained in a kind of deposit-box, to which church authorises held the key. The quotations again speak for themselves:

... Everything that is contrary to the sound teaching that goes with the Good News. (1 Timothy 1:10)

The church of the living God upholds the truth and keeps it safe. (3:15)

Anyone... who does not keep to the sound teaching which is that of our Lord Jesus Christ... is simply ignorant. (6:3)

My dear Timothy, take great care of all that has been entrusted to you. (6:20)

I know who it is that I have put my trust in, and I have no doubt at all that he is able to take care of all that has been entrusted to me. (2 Timothy 1:12)

Keep as your pattern the sound teaching you have heard from me. (1:13)

You have been trusted to look after something precious; guard it. (1:14)

You have heard everything that I teach in public; hand it on to reliable people so that they in turn will be able to teach others. (2:2)

You must keep to what you have been taught. (3:13)

Far from being content with sound teaching, people will be avid for the latest novelty. (4:3)

(The elder) must have a firm grasp of the unchanging message of the tradition, so that he can be counted on for both expounding the sound doctrine and refuting those who argue against it. (Titus 1:9)

Be severe in correcting them, and make them sound in the faith. (1:13)

Preach the behaviour that goes with healthy doctrine. The older men should be... sound in faith. (2:1)

When you are teaching... keep all that you say so wholesome that nobody can make any objections to it. (2:7)

Here is a saying that you can rely on... 'Jesus Christ came into the world to save sinners.' (1 Timothy 1:15)

Here is a saying that you can rely on: 'To want to be a presiding elder is to want to do a noble work.' (3:1)

'The usefulness of spirituality is unlimited'... that is a saying that you can rely on. (4:8–9)

Here is a saying that you can rely on: 'If we have died with him then we shall live with him...' (2 Timothy 2:11)

'We are justified by grace, and heirs looking forward to inheriting eternal life.' This is doctrine that you can rely on. (Titus 3:8)

Institutionalisation

The church organisation necessary for handing on the kind of static 'truth' here envisaged is correspondingly more rigid than anything that we have seen previously in Paul's letters.

From the Acts of the Apostles, we know that the earliest missions were presided over by the individual apostle who founded a Christian community in a given area. When he passed on to other mission fields he left behind a group of 'elders' to be responsible to him from the distance. From early church history we know that, by the second century, each local community had its own permanent 'president' or bishop, assisted by a group of 'elders'.

Here, at a stage halfway between the two, we find what is probably to be expected. The apostle no longer assumes responsibility for the mission; he has delegated this to Timothy and Titus, who are assisted by a group of indistinguishable 'elders and presidents'. On the other hand, they remain responsible for several communites and not only one, and are not appointed in any kind of permanent way. Presumably, as they move on elsewhere, responsiblity for the individual communities will devolve on one member of the group of 'elders', who will eventually assume the title of 'president' or bishop. Perhaps the church could only grow by building such structures for itself. But they bring with them the shadows of institutionalisation, so refreshingly absent from the earlier letters of Paul.

These gradually hardening structures are perhaps responsible for the many references in these letters to the future Day of the Coming or Appearing of Christ. It is as if the optimistic vision of the Captivity Epistles, of a Christ coming into everyday living and of an eternal life enjoyed here and now, has been regretfully shelved in the light of harsh reality, and the earlier imagery brought back again, of a Christ who only comes at the end of time to reward those who have kept the faith:

Do all that you have been told, with no faults or failures,
until the Appearing of our Lord Jesus Christ.
(1 Timothy 6:14)

Tell (the rich) that they are to be generous and willing to share – this is the way that they can save up a good capital sum for the future if they want to make sure of the only life that is real. (6:18–19)

I have no doubt at all that (God) is able to take care of all that has been entrusted to me until that Day. (2 Timothy 1:12)

May (Onesiphorus) find the Lord's mercy on that Day. (1:18)

In the end may they (the chosen) have the salvation that is in Christ Jesus and the eternal glory that comes with it. (2:10)

Before Christ Jesus who is to be judge of the living and the dead, I put this duty to you, in the name of his Appearing. (4:1)

The crown of righteousness reserved for me, which the Lord, the righteous judge, will give me on that Day; and not only to me but to all those who have longed for his Appearing. (4:8)

The Lord will... bring me safely to his heavenly kingdom. (4:18)

We are waiting in hope for the blessing which will come with the Appearing of our saviour Christ Jesus. (Titus 2:13)

Jewels

Yet this must not be my last word on these letters, lest I seem to have damned them entirely. For they contain within them two passages that shine out like jewels.

The first is such a fine summary of the gospel Paul made his own that it is no wonder it has been chosen as one of the readings for the Christmas liturgy. Like much of Paul's writing, it has a lyrical quality which can perhaps best be conveyed by setting it out as a poem:

When the kindness of God our saviour
and his love for mankind were revealed,
it was not because he was concerned
with any religous actions

we might have done ourselves;
it was for no reason
except his own compassion that he saved us,
by means of the cleansing water of rebirth,
and by renewing us with the Holy Spirit
which he has so generously poured over us
through Jesus Christ our saviour.
He did this
so that we should be justified by his grace,
to become heirs
looking forward to inheriting eternal life. (Titus 3:4–7)

The second has no need to have its poetic quality pointed out. It seems to be an existing hymn which is quoted to illustrate how deep is the 'mystery of our religion'. The mystery is left unexplained; it is simply specified in six lines of no more than two or three words apiece. Literally these lines run:

Manifested in the flesh,
Vindicated in the Spirit,
Seen by angels,
Proclaimed to the nations,
Believed on in the world,
Taken up in glory.

These enigmatic lines obviously need a little elaboration if their import is to be conveyed to the ordinary reader. I have done this in what follows, taking the six lines as three couplets, each making one of the three following stanzas:

He was born, as you or I,
In a body which must die,
Yet his death was not for ever, he lives on.
Who is this, as you or I,
Who was born to live and die,
Yet his death was not for ever, he lives on?
  Deep, deep, deep is the mystery I sing,
  Dark, dark, dark is the riddle:
  He was born, as you or I,
  In a body which must die,
  Yet his death was not for ever, he lives on.

Not a soul, so it is said,
Saw him raised up from the dead,

Yet by now the story's known throughout the world.
Who is this whom it is said,
No one saw raised from the dead,
Yet by now the story's known throughout the world?
   Deep, deep, deep is the mystery I sing,
   Dark, dark, dark is the riddle:
   Not a soul, so it said,
   Saw him raised up from the dead,
   Yet by now the story's known throughout the world.

His believers, when they've met,
Know he's there with them, and yet
He's with God – what makes us think that's somewhere else?
Who is this who, when they've met,
Is right there with them, and yet
He's with God – what makes us think that's somewhere else?
   Deep, deep, deep is the mystery I sing,
   Dark, dark, dark is the riddle:
   His believers, when they've met,
   Know he's there with them, and yet
   He's with God – what makes us think that's somewhere
   else?
(1 Timothy 3:16, authors version)

This magnificent expression of the Christian mystery can bear comparison with any page of Paul's letters.

FOR DISCUSSION

1. This chapter has criticised the excessive concern these letters show for 'orthodoxy'. Could a Christian community more intent on right behaviour than on right doctrine go astray?

2. Is the gradual institutionalisation of any new movement to be welcomed, to be deplored, or simply to be accepted as inevitable?

3. The excerpt from the letter to Titus on p.134 has emphasised a favourite theme of Paul's, that we are saved by faith not by works, by God's goodness not by our own. Does this teaching make you feel good or bad? Does it make you feel less responsible or more?

ST PAUL'S LETTERS IN ORDER

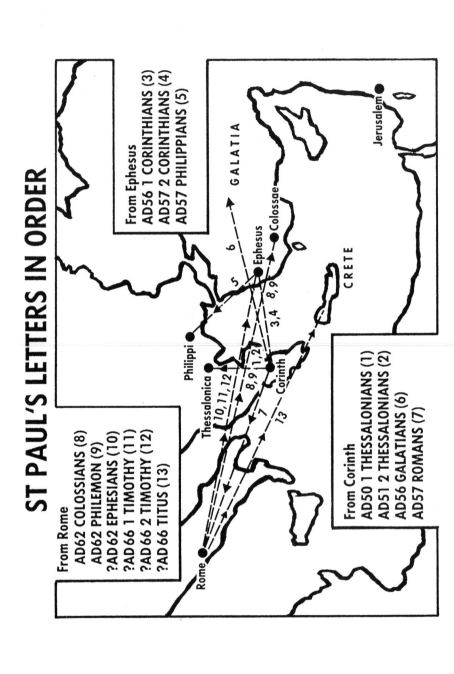

From Rome
AD62 COLOSSIANS (8)
AD62 PHILEMON (9)
?AD62 EPHESIANS (10)
?AD66 1 TIMOTHY (11)
?AD66 2 TIMOTHY (12)
?AD66 TITUS (13)

From Ephesus
AD56 1 CORINTHIANS (3)
AD57 2 CORINTHIANS (4)
AD57 PHILIPPIANS (5)

From Corinth
AD50 1 THESSALONIANS (1)
AD51 2 THESSALONIANS (2)
AD56 GALATIANS (6)
AD57 ROMANS (7)

GALATIA

CRETE

Jerusalem

Ephesus

Colossae

Philippi

Thessalonica

Corinth

Rome